The Cult
of the Virgin

CRI *Books*

Jehovah's Witnesses, Jesus Christ, and the Gospel of John, Robert M. Bowman, Jr.

A Crash Course on the New Age Movement: Describing and Evaluating a Growing Social Force, Elliot Miller

Why You Should Believe in the Trinity, Robert M. Bowman, Jr.

The Counterfeit Christ of the New Age Movement, Ron Rhodes

Understanding Jehovah's Witnesses: Why They Read the Bible the Way They Do, Robert M. Bowman, Jr.

UFOs in the New Age: Extraterrestrial Messages and the Truth of Scripture, William M. Alnor

The Cult of the Virgin: Catholic Mariology and the Apparitions of Mary, Elliot Miller & Kenneth R. Samples

---

Elliot Miller is editor-in-chief of publications for the Christian Research Institute (CRI), an evangelical investigative organization. He is author of *A Crash Course on the New Age Movement,* has served as a major contributor to two books, and has also written several pamphlets, articles, and fact sheets dealing with new religious movements, apologetics, and doctrinal controversies. In addition to his literary work, he is an ordained minister and has served as a pastor and Bible teacher. He holds a B.A. in ministry from Anaheim Christian College and an M.A. in apologetics from the Simon Greenleaf School of Law.

Kenneth R. Samples is senior research consultant at the Christian Research Institute. He is also a college instructor who has written for numerous publications, and a popular speaker, regularly featured on the radio program "The Bible Answer Man." He has an M.A. in systematic theology from Talbot School of Theology and is now pursuing advanced studies in philosophy.

The Cult of the Virgin

Catholic Mariology and the Apparitions of Mary

Elliot Miller
and Kenneth R. Samples

Foreword by Norman L. Geisler
Response by Mitchell Pacwa, S.J.

BAKER BOOK HOUSE
Grand Rapids, Michigan 49516

Library of Congress Cataloging-in-Publication Data

Miller, Elliot.
   The cult of the Virgin : Catholic Mariology and the apparitions of Mary / Elliot
   Miller and Kenneth R. Samples ; foreword by Norman Geisler.
      p.   cm.
   Includes bibliographical references and index.
   ISBN 0-8010-6291-8
   1. Mary, Blessed Virgin, Saint—Theology. 2. Mary, Blessed Virgin, Saint—
   Apparitions and miracles. I. Samples, Kenneth R.
   II. Title.
   BT613.M56 1992
   232.91—dc20   92-4273

Much of the content of this book originally appeared in the *Christian Research Journal*
between Summer 1990 and Spring 1991. (For subscription information write: Christian
Research Institute, P.O. Box 500, San Juan Capistrano, CA 92693-0500.)

Photos on pages 117–20 taken by Paul Carden

This book is fondly dedicated to the memory of
Walter Martin
founder of the Christian Research Institute.
It was he who first modeled for us
a balanced approach to Roman Catholicism.
He freely acknowledged that there are
many true Christians
and much that is orthodox within the Catholic church,
but he did not gloss over
the serious differences that remain
between Catholics and Protestants.

Contents

Contents

Acknowledgments

We are indebted in many ways to our co-workers and friends at the Christian Research Institute (CRI). Ron Rhodes and Robert M. Bowman, Jr., made valuable editorial contributions to the articles on which this book is based. Researcher Paul Carden's persistence helped open several doors for interviews in Medjugorje. CRI President Hank Hanegraaff's enthusiasm for and belief in this project helped make the trip to Medjugorje possible. We thank the many supporters of CRI who overwhelmingly responded to our appeal for help in financing the trip.

Foreword

The Bible speaks of the Virgin Mary as "the mother of my Lord" (Luke 1:43), and orthodox Christian creeds speak of Mary as the "Mother of God." Indeed, she was the mother of the one person who is both God and man, the Lord Jesus Christ. Both Catholic and Protestant theologians agree that Mary is a created person and, as such, should not receive worship that is due to God alone. Both agree that she is the most blessed of all women, having been chosen of God to be the earthly mother of our heavenly Savior (Luke 1:28).

It is here, however, that the points of agreement come to an end. And, in an ecumenical age it may seem appropriate to leave well enough alone. Why stress differences when there are such important similarities? Why go on and point out—as the authors of this book do—the many doctrines that separate Catholic Mariology from what Protestants consider the biblical view? There are several reasons, each of which involves concerns which extend far beyond a doctrine of Mary per se.

First of all, the Roman Catholic doctrine on Mary has gone well beyond Holy Scripture. But even the great Catholic theologian Thomas Aquinas affirmed that "only the canonical Scriptures are normative for faith" (*Commentary on John* 21, lect. 6). In going beyond Scripture in their teachings about Mary, Roman Catholics have threatened Scripture as the sole authority for the faith. This is one reason why those dedicated to the principle of *Sola Scriptura* cannot avoid addressing this issue.

Second, in exalting Mary beyond her divinely appointed role as the blessed earthly mother of our Lord, many Catholics have diminished the unique role of Christ in salvation. Thus another sensitive area is invaded, which Protestants have called *Solus Christus*. For orthodox Protestants, Christ and Christ alone is the Savior and Mediator between God and man (1 Tim. 2:5). Hence, the authors of this book rightly feel obligated to point out the gulf between what the Roman Catholic hierarchy officially says about Mary and what many Roman Catholic lay believers actually do.

The authors are to be commended for an honest evaluation of the differences between Catholic and Protestant thought on Mary. They are also to be praised for their openness to dialogue with Catholics on these points of tension. While all can agree with the dictum, "In essentials unity, in nonessentials liberty, and in all things charity," exactly what is "essential" and what is not must remain open to discussion. Catholics may be willing to grant that their beliefs concerning Mary are not essentials of the faith (at least not necessary for salvation). But, as the authors demonstrate, there are aspects of Catholic Mariology—the veneration of Mary and her exalted position as coredemptrix and mediatrix with Christ—which negatively affect other doctrines that *are* essential. Furthermore, the dogma of her bodily assumption into heaven and belief in her exaltation as the "Queen of heaven" seem little more than baptized paganism to many Protestants (see, e.g., Jer. 7:18).

On the other hand, it is fair to say—as the authors point out—that Mary has hardly been given her God-appointed respect in most Protestant circles as the "favored one" of the Lord (Luke 1:28). While many Catholics overexalt Mary, many Protestants do not even see her correctly as the most blessed among women (Luke 1:42).

This book is a friendly but frank effort to lay this ecumenical thorn on the table. It deserves a wide reading and serious attention from both sides of the theological fence.

Norman L. Geisler

INTRODUCTION

The Cult of the Virgin Revives

On March 25, 1987, Pope John Paul II issued an encyclical (papal letter) on the Virgin Mary in preparation for a fourteen-month "Marian year" that began the following June. Paradoxically, the encyclical called on all Christians (not just Roman Catholics) to accept Mary as a source of *unity* amongst themselves, because she is their "common mother."[1] The Pope's proclamation could be viewed as a paradox because his two predecessors, John XXIII and Paul VI, had deliberately *de-emphasized* Mary for the sake of promoting unity with their "separated brethren."[2]

Although the twentieth century has been characterized by at least one church historian as "the most active age of devotion to the Virgin,"[3] the cult of the Virgin reached a low ebb after the 1962–65 Second Vatican Council (using here the definition of "cult" which indicates obsessive devotion to or veneration for a person, principle, or ideal). The ecumenism unleashed by that council led the church hierarchy to assume a more restrained posture on Mary. At the same time, a general lapse in Marian fervor became evident among the laity, particularly in America and Canada. "Her statues disappeared from the sanctuaries of many Catholic churches; traditional hymns to her were no longer sung. Theologians lost interest in Marian doctrines. A generation of Catholic schoolchildren grew up without learning how to say the Rosary."[4]

Ecumenism prospered. The post-Vatican II church's emphases on Christ and Scripture caused many Protestants to rethink their position that the Roman Catholic Church is "cultic" or "apostate." Movements such as the Charismatic Renewal and Cursillo (three days in Christian community aimed at spiritual renewal) produced a new breed of "born-again Catholics," shocking evangelicals with their obvious devotion to Christ as personal Savior. Dialogues between Catholics and various Protestant bodies led many on both sides to wonder if perhaps the gaps between them were not impassable after all.[5]

Enter Pope John Paul II, the former bishop of Krakow, Poland, whose lifelong devotion to Mary is expressed by his blue and white shield bearing the letter *M*, and by his motto, *Totus Tuus sum Maria* (Latin for "Mary, I am all yours").[6] Soon after ascending to the papal throne in 1978 he launched a campaign to revive the cult of Mary in the church. Before a watching world he visited almost all of her notable shrines, weeping in prayer before her grotto at Lourdes, France. He inaugurated the above-mentioned Marian year, which encouraged liturgical services in her honor and pilgrimages to her shrines. He gave Mary credit for his recovery from one assassination attempt and for his escape from a second one unscathed. He believes she is responsible for the disintegration of communism in Eastern Europe.

Such concerted efforts to rekindle the flame of Marian devotion were bound to meet with some success, considering the immense popularity of John Paul II. But the flame he ignited now threatens to become a roaring fire, thanks largely to the wide acceptance of Mary's reputed daily apparitions in Medjugorje, Yugoslavia. Mary is now "back in style." As *Time* reported in a late 1991 cover story, "A grass-roots revival of faith in the Virgin is taking place worldwide. Millions of worshipers are flocking to her shrines, many of them young people. . . . The late 20th century has become the age of the Marian pilgrimage."[7] Moreover, "Marian scholarship and writings are on the rise. The rosary is increasing in popularity . . . claims of apparitions of Mary are on a worldwide upswing."[8]

The time has come for a Protestant response. Just as surely as a man cannot "take fire in his bosom, and his clothes not be burned" (Prov. 6:27), Catholics cannot renew their emphasis on Mary without injuring ecumenism. Their view of Mary is not the only issue that separates Catholics from Protestants, to be sure. Other issues, such as authority (i.e., the proper relationship between Scripture and the church) and the nature of justification, are more fundamental. Nonetheless, Marian dogma and devotion probably cut to the Protestant quick more rapidly than anything else. When a Catholic breaks out in prayer to or in praise of the "most holy mother of God," the typical Protestant response is, "Let me out of here!"

The purpose of part 1 of this book is to explain in detail why Protestants consider the Catholic Mary to be unhistorical and unbiblical. While this may appear antiecumenical, it is ultimately the opposite. For if issues and concerns such as those raised here are not openly addressed, dialogue and communion between Catholics and Protestants (at least evangelicals) will inevitably reach an impasse. Our focus here will be on the distinguishing theological features of Catholic Mariology.

The issue of Medjugorje in particular and Marian apparitions in general (including the prophetic messages they convey and the devotional practices that have allegedly resulted from them, such as the rosary and scapulars) will be examined in part 2 of this book.

Part II

From Lowly Handmaid to Queen of Heaven: The Mary of Roman Catholic Theology

Elliot Miller

1

Divine Maternity

To understand the development of Catholic Mariology it is vital to grasp the significance of what happened at the Council of Chalcedon in A.D. 451. At this council the church officially assigned the title *Theotokos* ("God-bearer" or "mother of God") to Mary. The original intent behind the title, which was first employed in the fourth century by such church fathers as Athanasius and Gregory Nazianzen, was not to exalt Mary. After the Council of Nicaea (A.D. 325), where the church officially confessed its belief that Christ is truly God, the question of how his deity relates to his humanity quite naturally presented itself. Over the following century a great controversy grew in which speculative attempts to reconcile this theological problem were presented, none of which satisfied the majority of the faithful.

One hotly debated theory, identified with Nestorius, the bishop of Constantinople, contended that the divine Word and the man Jesus were two separate persons. The two became united when the human Jesus was assumed into the being of the divine Word; that

19

is, the divine Word clothed himself with the man Jesus. (It is not certain whether Nestorius actually held this view, but his followers, the Nestorians, did.) The orthodox rightly rejected this Christology, sensing that, while the Scriptures indeed teach (albeit, not in technical theological terms) that Jesus Christ possesses two distinct natures, the two natures concur in one eternal person.

In his preaching Nestorius consistently used the title "Mother of Christ" for Mary. Suspecting a theological motivation was implicit in the title, the orthodox emphatically insisted that Mary is the mother of God. By this they meant to uphold the truths that the man born of Mary was truly God, and, conversely, that the second person in the Godhead had indeed taken upon himself the full nature of man. At the Council of Chalcedon this dogma was defined thus: "This selfsame one was born of Mary the virgin, who is God-bearer (*Theo-tokos*) in respect of his human-ness (*anthropoteta*)."[1]

But there were in the church at that time other threats to biblical truth besides Nestorianism. Cults of devotees to Mary and to various other saints already existed on the periphery of the church. When the Council of Chalcedon in 451 officially recognized Mary as the mother of God, opportunity was allowed for the cult of the Virgin to infiltrate the mainstream of the church.

As chapter 7 will reveal in more detail, the religious life of the Greco-Roman world was largely founded upon devotion to various deities associated with fertility, particularly goddesses. When the Roman Empire was nominally converted to Christianity under Constantine and his successors, this devotion was idolatrously transferred to Mary and the saints. (Although many anti-Catholics have overstated the influence of paganism on the church, such influence is nonetheless relevant to the present discussion, as I will demonstrate in chapter 7.) No doubt there existed a desire on the part of some to exalt Mary to the highest heavens, and after the title Mother of God was assigned to her, such a process began in earnest. The sentiment grew that, because of her divine maternity,

From Lowly Handmaid to Queen of Heaven

Mary transcended all other created beings and stood next to her exalted Son in heavenly glory.

There is no question that the entire array of Catholic doctrines concerning Mary issued out of the church's unreserved pronouncement that she is *Theotokos*, mother of God. In the words of prominent American Mariologist Eamon R. Carroll:

> The cornerstone had been placed by this definition of dogma for the subsequent development of Mariology. The intimate bond between the *Theotokos* and the God-Man was indicative of the trend the developing Mariology would take. . . . The Church in ages to come would discover the deeper treasures of the divine Maternity, for in the words of Pius XII, "from this sublime office of the Mother of God seem to flow, as it were from a most limpid hidden source, all the privileges and graces with which her soul and life were adorned to such extraordinary manner and measure."[2]

Natures Do Not Have Mothers

If the designation of Mary as mother of God at Chalcedon gave rise to the exaltation of her that followed, we would do well to examine exactly how biblical this title is. Catholic theologians argue that since Jesus is truly God, and Mary truly gave birth to him, then quite naturally Mary is the mother of God. As Catholic apologist Frank Sheed puts it, "Do not think it is sufficient to call her the mother of his human nature; natures . . . do not have mothers. She was mother, as yours or mine is, of the person born of her. And the person was God the Son."[3]

Sheed's point is well taken. Though some Protestants have disputed any use of the term, in the sense that the person she gave birth to is—by identity—God, Mary is the mother of God. To give her the title without immediate qualification, however, is irresponsible and potentially misleading. The natural interpretation of an unconstrained wielding of the term would be that the eternal

God has a mother. The God of the Bible, who has always existed and who created all things, has no mother. The second person of this Triune Deity, who in time and space became united to a human nature in the Virgin's womb, looks to Mary as mother with respect to his manhood, not with respect to his godhood.

Furthermore, in all other cases of motherhood, children can look to their mothers and fathers as the source from which their existence sprang. However, in this case the Son existed before his mother, and, in fact, she owes her existence to him (John 1:1–2).

Clearly, the term *mother of God* can only be applied to Mary in one narrow sense. It therefore follows that to use it without strict qualification will naturally result in serious confusion, especially to the theologically unschooled. Since it is nearly impossible always to make such clarifications when using a title, it is no wonder that the authors of Scripture refrained from calling Mary the mother of God, choosing rather to call her the mother of Jesus (e.g., John 2:1). We should learn from their example, while we at the same time maintain with the Council of Chalcedon that the one she bore is definitely God.

Nearer My God to Thee?

Another inference Catholics draw from the divine maternity is expressed by respected Catholic theologian Ludwig Ott: "As the mother of God, Mary transcends in dignity all created persons, angels and men, because the dignity of a creature is the greater the nearer it is to God. . . . As a true mother she is related by blood to the Son of God according to His human nature."[4]

Does Mary's physical relationship to Jesus really elevate her to such an exalted position? Biblically we can go so far as to say that Mary was and is blessed among women (Luke 1:42). But this is due more to the important role she was elected to play (bringing the Messiah into the world) than the mere fact of a physical relationship. Actually, with what would appear to be divine foresight,

From Lowly Handmaid to Queen of Heaven

Jesus consistently sought to counter the natural human tendency to esteem *carnal* relationship with him higher than *spiritual* (Matt. 12:46–50; Luke 11:27–28; 2:48–50). Rather than emphasize his physical relationship with his mother, he seemed to go out of his way to downplay it, even calling her woman (John 2:1–4; 19:26), which (as noted Mariologist Michael O'Carroll acknowledges[5]) was not a customary address for a Jewish son to use. Furthermore, Paul and the other New Testament authors do nothing to counter this impression that Mary is not to be exalted on the grounds of her physical relationship to Christ. We must therefore conclude that the later tendency to exalt Mary on such grounds is not only unsupported by Scripture, it runs counter to it.

2

Perpetual Virginity

At the Second Council of Constantinople (A.D. 553), the church used the phrase *ever virgin* (Greek: *aeiparthenos*) with reference to Mary. Although by this time the formula "A virgin conceived, a virgin gave birth, a virgin remained" was almost universally accepted, such had not always been the case. Several early church fathers (including Tertullian) had rejected this view,[1] and it was a subject of intense debate as late as the fourth century (an example of this debate, involving "Pope" Siricius, is referred to below).

As almost all historians (including those of the Catholic church) recognize, the eventual doctrinal triumph of Mary's perpetual virginity was directly related to the rise of asceticism and monasticism. These traditions, which greatly influenced the medieval church and its developing Mariology, revered celibacy as being more inherently spiritual than the married state.

Is celibacy actually a higher spiritual state than marriage, as many Catholics have supposed? For that matter, is asceticism truly a biblical tradition? A historical survey will enlighten our consideration of these questions.

In the Old Testament we find the ideal woman of virtue set forth as a faithful wife and homemaker (Prov. 31). While childbearing (within marriage) is exalted (Ps. 127:3–5; 1 Sam. 1:11), celibacy is never advocated.

It is true that in the New Testament Paul recommends celibacy for some (1 Cor. 7), but he does so for practical reasons (vv. 26, 28, 32–35), not because of some inherently superior virtue and purity in the celibate state. Rather, the New Testament reiterates and even expands on the Old Testament's positive depiction of the marital union: it was instituted by God (Matt. 19:6); it is to be held in great honor (Heb. 13:4); it is a "type" of the relationship between Christ and his church (Eph. 5:31–32).

By contrast, in the Platonically influenced philosophies that permeated the Roman Empire, the material world was often viewed as being intrinsically evil. Thus, those who were of a religious bent would often shun material pleasures—particularly sexual relations in or out of marriage—as being wholly opposed to spiritual growth. The material world was seen by many as the creation of a fallen being crudely comparable to the biblical Satan.

This Gnostic kind of philosophy so influenced the church that even today many Protestants are not free of the notion that the material world is inherently evil. Yet, this is totally unbiblical. The Bible reveals that God created all things, including the material world and sex, and pronounced that they were all good, very good (see Gen. 1). It is only when human beings through their free wills irresponsibly pervert the natural use God intended for the things in his creation that evil becomes associated with them (e.g., sex outside of marriage, drug and alcohol dependency, gluttony, greed).

Operating under the assumption that there is something inherently defiling about sexual relations, defenders of Mary's perpetual virginity have invoked not only the honor of Mary but that of Christ as well. Siricius, whom the Catholic church looks back to as one of the early popes (A.D. 384–399), intervened in a dispute between Anysius, bishop of Thessalonica, and Bonosus, bishop in Illyria, and wrote to Anysius: "You had good reason to be horrified at the thought that another birth might issue from the same virginal womb from which Christ was born according to the flesh. For the Lord Jesus would never have chosen to be born of a virgin if He had ever judged that she would be so incontinent as to contaminate with the seed of human intercourse the birthplace of the Lord's body, that court of the Eternal King."[2]

Siricius no doubt took this position out of true honor for Christ, but he was missing one of the most important points of the incarnation. While Christ is most certainly deserving of all glory and honor as eternal King, his purpose in becoming a man was to identify with humanity in all respects, excepting sin, so that he might be a true mediator between man and God (Heb. 4:15–16). Thus, according to Philippians 2:5–8, Christ in the incarnation voluntarily emptied himself of his kingly glory and humbled himself not only by becoming a man but by becoming a servant to men. His voluntary humility was signified for the world by his birth in a manger. Since there is nothing defiling about sexual relations within marriage, to suggest that Christ would not want to be conceived in a womb that would later conceive other humans is to take away from the glory that God would afterward give him for the very fact of his voluntary humility (Phil. 2:9–11).

What Does Scripture Say?

Catholic and Protestant theological concerns aside, the most important question is, What does Scripture say? Biblically, it would seem clear enough that Mary had normal marital relations with Joseph after the birth of Jesus (Matt. 1:18, 25), and that this was in keeping with God's will for the couple (1 Cor. 7:3–5). Perhaps the strongest evidence to this effect is the repeated reference to the "brothers and sisters" of Jesus, including Matthew 13:55–56 and Mark 6:3, where the brothers are mentioned by name.

The Catholic church's traditional interpretation of these verses is represented for us by lay Catholic apologist Karl Keating. He cites several examples in the Old Testament where the Hebrew equivalent of "brother" is used with reference to a cousin, or even someone more remotely related. The Hebrew did not have a word for "cousin," Keating points out, and neither did the Aramaic, which Jesus and his disciples spoke. He argues that, although the Greek did have a word for "cousin" *(anepsios)*, it was common for Jews writing in Greek to continue the Hebrew practice of referring to all relatives as brothers, which in the Greek is *adelphos*. He cites examples of this from the Septuagint (a Greek translation of the Hebrew Scriptures, produced in the third century B.C.) and claims that "the same usage was employed by the writers of the New Testament."[3] Hence, Jesus' "brothers and sisters" need only be cousins.

There is one conspicuous ingredient missing from Keating's argument: he never gives an example of a New Testament writer using *adelphos* for a cousin. The fact that the Septuagint did so does not establish that the contemporary narratives and letters of the New Testament must also have done so. After all, it would be natural for the Septuagint, a translation of the Hebrew Scriptures, to follow the usage employed in those Scriptures, even if that usage had since been dropped with the changing of languages and the passing of time. The reason he fails to provide this important evidence for his case is obvious: there are no such examples.

Keating's case is further weakened by the fact that *anepsios* is used in the New Testament. In Colossians 4:10 Paul refers to "Mark, the cousin [*anepsios*] of Barnabas."

Accordingly, there is no reason not to think that "Jesus' brothers [*adelphos*] and sisters" means exactly what it appears to mean. This is strongly supported by the fact that the "brethren" of Jesus are usually mentioned as being with Mary, as though they were in her immediate family.

Furthermore, while Abraham, for example, called his nephew, Lot, a brother in Genesis 13:8, in other places Scripture makes it clear that Lot was not Abraham's literal brother. No such clarification is made regarding Jesus' brethren in the New Testament. If Mary's perpetual virginity is true, and if it is as important a dogma as the Roman church insists, then certainly the evangelists, writing under the influence of the Holy Spirit, would have clarified the matter.

No Knowledge of Man

Keating provides a battery of scriptural arguments in favor of Mary's perpetual virginity, only one of which, in my judgment, merits our attention here: "At the Annunciation, when the angel Gabriel appeared to Mary, she asked, 'How can that be, since I have no knowledge of man?' (Luke 1:34). From the earliest interpretations of the Bible we see that this was taken to mean that she had made a vow of lifelong virginity, even in marriage. If she had taken no such vow, the question would make no sense at all."[4]

In reply, I must first point out what Mary did not say. She did not respond, "How can this be, since I will never have knowledge of man?"; or, ". . . since I have made a permanent vow of celibacy?" At the time of the annunciation, and for several months to come (until the predetermined time arrived for her marriage to Joseph to be consummated), she certainly did "have no knowledge of man." To maintain the Protestant view, then, we need only infer that Mary understood the angel to mean that the promised conception would occur in the very near future.

Is this a necessary inference? It is if we consider that the alternative creates far more interpretive problems than it solves. Keating's suggestion that Mary took "a vow of lifelong virginity, even in marriage," proposes something unheard of and unthinkable in biblical culture. For the Jews then—even as in our own culture today—a marriage that remained unconsummated would not for

From Lowly Handmaid to Queen of Heaven

long be considered a marriage. With typical Reformation-era acerbity, John Calvin puts the matter in perspective: "She would, in that case, have committed treachery by allowing herself to be united to a husband, and would have poured contempt on the holy covenant of marriage. . . . Although the Papists have exercised barbarous tyranny on this subject, yet they have never proceeded so far as to allow the wife to form a vow of continence at her own pleasure."[5]

3

The Immaculate Conception

Building one dogma on another, the church reasoned that it was not enough for Mary—as the mother of God—to have been pure in body; she must also have been pure in soul. In the words of Eamon R. Carroll:

> Once the divine Maternity and the perpetual virginity of Mary had been proposed by the church's teaching authority as true Catholic doctrine, the way was open for further development. . . . Belief in Mary's virginity led to an emphasis on her holiness. The experience of the ascetics first showed the connection between a life of perpetual virginity and holiness. But still deeper reflection was needed to appreciate the full treasure of Mary's sanctity, and this came through reflection on the divine Maternity. From the divine motherhood had come the awareness of perfect virginity; now Christian thought saw that God would make his Mother all-perfect, by gifts of grace beyond compare.[1]

The doctrine of Mary's sinlessness emerged gradually. Several Greek church fathers (e.g., Origen,[2] John Chrysostom, Cyril of Alexandria, and Basil) held that Mary, although outstandingly holy in character, had nonetheless been guilty of such sins as doubt, vanity, and ambition.[3] However, the Syrian Ephram (306–373) said: "Mary and Eve were two people without guilt. Later one became the cause of our death, the other the cause of our life."[4] Following Ephram, the Latin fathers refrained from charging Mary with sin. Ambrose of Milan idealized Mary as the perfect virgin. Augustine, who had been strongly influenced by Ambrose, taught that while Mary (like all humans) had been conceived with original sin, she received a special measure of grace through which she overcame it.

By maintaining that Mary was free from *personal* sin, Augustine helped propel the church toward eventually maintaining that she was free from *original* sin. Thus, the position he so passionately defended against Pelagius—that Adam's original sin was passed on to all his children—would be undermined by his own influence. Nonetheless, as Carroll observes, "Many more centuries of thought and prayer were required before the Church would realize that the Immaculate Conception was among the gifts God provided for his Mother."[5]

The doctrine that Mary was conceived "immaculately"—without the stain of original sin—was first propagated at the beginning of the twelfth century by the British monk Eadmer.[6] It was strongly opposed, however, by virtually all the leading theologians of the time, including Thomas Aquinas, Bonaventure, Peter Lombard, and Alexander of Hales. They warned that the doctrine contradicts the biblically revealed truths of the universality of sin and the need of all people to be saved.

A major portion of the credit for establishing the immaculate conception as Catholic dogma goes to John Duns Scotus (1264–1308). He argued that to hold that Mary was preserved from original sin would not depreciate the atonement but rather would magnify it: it would be an even greater work of redemptive grace for Mary to be born without sin than to be given the power to rise above it. In other words, sanctifying grace derived from the foreseen merits of Christ enabled Mary to escape the original sin that, as a member of Adam's race, she otherwise would have inherited.

All the same, the doctrine remained controversial (especially in the fourteenth and fifteenth centuries) until Pope Pius IX defined it as unquestionable dogma in 1854. In declaring the first dogma ever to be pronounced solely on the authority of a pope without the official sanction of a council, Pius IX stated:

> We pronounce, declare and define . . . that the doctrine which holds the Blessed Virgin Mary to have been, from the first moment of her conception, by a singular grace and privilege of Almighty God, in view of the merits of Christ Jesus the Saviour of mankind, preserved free from all stain of original sin, was revealed by God, and is, therefore, to be firmly and constantly believed by all the faithful.[7]

The church holds that as a result of the immaculate conception, Mary possesses all gifts, knowledge, and fruits in their fullness, and is exalted above all men and angels.

"Hail, Full of Grace"

The chief biblical text used in support of this doctrine is Luke 1:28, where in older English versions the angel Gabriel greets Mary: "Hail, full of grace [Greek: *kecharitomenē*]." O'Carroll observes that her

> fullness of grace . . . became a basic concept about her in theology. . . . It has been seen as the foundation of Mary's unique holiness and consequent sinlessness, and it has been proposed as the fundamental principle of all Marian theology.

32

Scholastic theologians have deduced from it the entire grouping of the theological and moral virtues, the Gifts of the Holy Spirit, and extraordinary graces and charisms [that Mary is believed to possess].[8]

O'Carroll and other contemporary Mariologists freely recognize, however, that "'full of grace' is a mistranslation, but in the Latin translation it influenced thinking on the subject."[9]

Luke 1:28 is still considered strong support for the immaculate conception, even if it was mistranslated. Keating presents this argument:

Newer translations, based directly on the Greek, render Luke 1:28 as "Rejoice, you who enjoy God's favor! The Lord is with you" (*New Jerusalem Bible*) or "Rejoice, O highly favored daughter! The Lord is with you." These translations are imperfect, since they give the impression that the favor bestowed on Mary was no different from that given other women in the Bible. . . .

The newer translations leave out something the Greek conveys, something the older translation conveys, which is that this grace (and the core of the word *kecharitomenē* is *charis*, after all) is at once permanent and of a singular kind. The Greek indicates a perfection of grace. A perfection must be perfect not only intensively, but extensively. The grace Mary enjoyed must not only have been as "full" or strong or complete as possible at any given time, but it must have extended over the whole of her life, from conception. That is, she must have been in a state of sanctifying grace from the first moment of her existence to have been called "full of grace" or to have been filled with divine favor in a singular way. This is just what the doctrine of the Immaculate Conception holds.[10]

With all due respect for the fact that Mary was indeed favored above all other women, Keating is reading more into the participle *kecharitomenē* (derived from the verb *charitoō*) than its scanty New

Testament usage allows. *Charitō* is used of believers in Ephesians 1:6 without implying sinless perfection. There is hence nothing about Luke 1:28 that establishes the doctrine of the immaculate conception. That Mary was uniquely favored to be the mother of her Lord is the only necessary inference.

An additional proof text cited for the immaculate conception is Luke 1:42, in which Elizabeth, John the Baptist's mother, says to Mary: "Blest are you among women and blest is the fruit of your womb." Ludwig Ott contends that "the blessing of God which rests upon Mary is *made parallel* to the blessing of God which rests on Christ in His humanity. This parallelism suggests that Mary, just like Christ, was from the beginning of her existence, free from all sin" (emphasis added).[11]

Like Keating, Ott finds more in the text than the text itself will justify. The only clear parallel is that both Christ and his mother have been blessed. Since Christ alone is God and Savior, they quite obviously could not be blessed in the same qualitative way. A mutual sinlessness is neither explicitly stated nor necessarily implied in Elizabeth's words. Rather, Mary is "blessed" in being chosen as the mother of the Redeemer.

God Has "Imprisoned" *All*

The more one's theology is rooted in the Bible, the more difficulties one should see with the doctrine of the immaculate conception. Throughout Scripture, a consistent witness against the sin of man is given. In 1 Kings 8:46 we read that "there is no man who does not sin." Ecclesiastes 7:20 tells us "there is no man on earth so just as to do good and never sin." In the New Testament, Galatians 3:22 affirms: "Scripture has locked all things in under the constraint of sin."

Paul's letter to the Romans, which deals with sin and salvation in the greatest depth, has much to say about the universality of sin. He maintains that "all men have sinned and are deprived of the glory

From Lowly Handmaid to Queen of Heaven

of God" (3:23). He then explains the factors responsible for this truth in chapter 5: "Therefore, just as through one man sin entered the world and with sin death, death thus coming to all men inasmuch as all sinned . . ." (v. 12). We see then that the sinful condition is inherited by all men and women from the first man, Adam.

Scripture allows only one exception to this otherwise universal rule: Jesus Christ (Heb. 7:26). By virtue of his divine nature and his virgin birth (through which God, rather than a son of Adam, was his Father), Christ dwelt among us as one free from sin, standing out in all of history as the *only* human who perfectly represented the holy character of the Father (John 15:9).

The sinful nature that has passed through the human race has been so pervasive and inexorable that no one has been immune from it, not even the most godly figures in the Bible. It took nothing less than deity "invading" our world in human flesh to break its murderous grip on the human race.

It is the absolute universality of sin—the fact that besides Christ there could be no exceptions—that makes it such a devastating foe of the human race. To suggest, therefore, that even one other person besides Christ was born without sin is to diminish the tremendous significance of the incarnation.

Scripture is clear that it is God's will and way that all human beings be brought low, that when he exalts them it might be entirely and unmistakably on the basis of his mercy and not their worthiness. "God has imprisoned all in disobedience that he might have mercy on all" (Rom. 11:32). The doctrine of the immaculate conception violates this basic biblical principle—all the talk about how it would be an "even greater work of grace" notwithstanding.

4

The Assumption

If Mary was conceived without sin, then it would seem reasonable that the result of sin—death—would not be able to hold her, even as it was unable to hold her Son (Acts 2:24). This is precisely how the church reasoned. The doctrine of the immaculate conception has therefore supplied a basis for the doctrine of Mary's assumption (i.e., ascension of her resurrected body into heaven). Pope Pius IX stated: "[Mary] by an entirely unique privilege completely overcame sin by her Immaculate Conception, and as a result she was not subject to the law of remaining in the corruption of the grave, and she did not have to wait until the end of time for the redemption of her body."[1] In the year 1864 the same Pope wrote in a letter to Queen Isabella II of Spain: "There is not doubt that the Assumption, in the sense commonly believed by the body of the faithful, follows from the Immaculate Conception."[2]

Neither Scripture nor church tradition offers insight into the nature of Mary's departure from this world. "There was great curiosity among Christians concerning the life and death of Mary.

Since there was no authentic information, imagination ran wild creating legends."[3] By the fifth century, apocryphal material (known as the *Transitus*) appeared, which attempted to explain the death of Mary. The authors of this literature often sought to pass themselves off as original apostles or contemporaries of Mary. Catholic theologian Karl Rahner acknowledges that "at best it can only be considered as evidence of theological speculation about Mary, which has been given the form of an ostensibly historical account. This is how we must regard the reports about Mary's Assumption. . . . Otherwise, there is nothing of any historical value in such apocryphal works."[4]

The accounts are filled with fantastic, absurd miracles, are written in poor taste, and contain bad theology. Yet, historians recognize them to be the source from which the doctrine of Mary's assumption arose. Mariologist Alfred C. Rush observes:

> Accounts were written of her death and then writers speculated on the lot of Mary after death. Once there was an actual confrontation of the death of Mary, this latter problem had to be faced also. When this took place, the Christian sense of the writers of these accounts revolted against the idea that one so glorious as Mary suffered the corruption of the grave; hence they postulate a glorification of Mary. She who was extraordinary in life, they claim, was extraordinary in death.[5]

Thus we see that the doctrine of the assumption first appeared not in Scripture,[6] nor even in that first-century tradition which the church considers authoritative, but in mythical material spawned out of human sentiment and reasoning.

The Feast of the Assumption was appointed by Gregory I (540–604) for August 15. It replaced the feast of her dormition, or falling asleep, which had been celebrated on January 18 in the West.

Throughout the centuries the sentiment that Mary must have been assumed into heaven continued to grow among the masses, and pressure was increasingly brought to bear upon the church's "teaching authority" (bishops) to define the belief as dogma. This culminated in a campaign in the latter nineteenth and early twentieth centuries which presented to the papacy eight million lay and nearly one hundred thousand religious votes for the assumption.

Because of the near-unanimous agreement among both the teaching authority and laity that the doctrine should be made dogma, Pope Pius XII in 1950 took the dubious step of pronouncing something to be a matter of faith *ex cathedra* ("with authority," or "from the seat of St. Peter"), which admittedly lacked definite support from either Scripture or church tradition. In the first dogmatic pronouncement made by a pope since the First Vatican Council determined in 1870 that the pope is infallible in matters of faith and morals when he speaks *ex cathedra*, Pius XII said: "We pronounce, declare, and define it to be a divinely revealed dogma: that the Immaculate Mother of God, the ever Virgin Mary, having completed the course of her earthly life, was assumed body and soul into heavenly glory."[7]

Potuit, Decuit, Fecit

The actual basis for the doctrine of the assumption is a form of logic often employed in Catholic theology (it is also appealed to in support of the immaculate conception), and described thus:

Potuit, decuit, fecit.

God can do all things.

It is proper that it should be so (e.g., that Mary should be assumed).

Therefore God did it.

This theological approach was illustrated by Pius XII when, in defense of his decision to define the belief as dogma, he affirmed: "Since it was within his [Christ's] power to grant her this great honour, to preserve her from the corruption of the tomb, *we must believe*, [*sic*] that he really acted in this way" (emphasis in original).[8]

While God certainly will do what is proper, theologians who take this approach to doctrine overlook the fact that they assume *a priori* that they know what is proper to God. Isaiah 55:8–9 tells us that God's thoughts and ways are not the thoughts and ways of man. This is true, because unlike God man is bound by the limitations of a finite nature, and even more so because man's reasoning process has been distorted by sin.

Even Catholic theology recognizes that doctrine cannot be determined by mere human sensibilities. For example, the doctrine that the damned are eternally punished in hell may seem too severe to human sentiments, but Catholics recognize that sinful humans are in no position to pass judgment on a holy God's judgment of sin. If we cannot fully grasp the horrific evil of sin, how can we fully grasp the absolute justice in God's punishment of it? In their denial of eternal punishment and other orthodox doctrines the Jehovah's Witnesses are an excellent example of how far a group can move from God's revealed truth when they allow fallible human reason to supersede Scripture in determining doctrine.

A Matter of Authority

It must be noted that the real issue in this disagreement between Catholic and Protestant theology is the oldest issue: authority. I have written of this in a previous work,[9] and it would go beyond our present scope to delve into it now. I will point out, however, that although many Protestants earnestly long and pray for a day when the whole body of believers truly will be united, they never will be able to recognize another authority equal to Holy Scripture.

Jesus' profound judgment of the Pharisees and scribes comes to mind, when he told them that they "nullify God's word in favor of the traditions you have handed down" (Mark 7:13). Protestants contend that the church's first error is to regard its tradition as equal in authority to the Word of God; the second and perhaps more damaging error is for the church to "absolutize" its own interpretation of both.

If we ask why the church dogmatized the assumption we are told that it is a revealed truth, part of the "Deposit of the Faith," the entire truth revealed through Christ's apostles in Scripture and church tradition (see glossary). When we point to the fact that there is no mention of the assumption in either Scripture or tradition, we are assured that it must be there in some embryonic stage, otherwise the church would not have defined it as dogma. We find ourselves caught in circular reasoning: the dogma is true because the church defined it; the church defined it because it's true.

Once Mary is viewed as assumed into heaven and sitting at the right hand of her Son, the way is opened for even more troubling doctrines concerning her to evolve, doctrines which, in the Protestant view, directly detract from the place and role of Christ. These we must turn to in the remaining chapters of part 1.

5

Spiritual Motherhood

According to Roman Catholic theology, Mary, the mother of Jesus, is the most exalted of all God's creatures—angels and humans. In the preceding chapters we examined the Catholic foundational dogmas (unquestionable teachings) that provide the basis for this view. We argued that, with the exception of the divine maternity (the concept of Mary as the mother of God), which itself has been given unbiblical significance, none of these dogmas are biblical. But it must also be conceded that none of them are heretical: they do not directly contradict doctrines that are essential to biblical faith. However, they have provided a basis for further speculation about Mary: additional doctrines have been proposed by the church that complete the picture of her exaltation. While the church's teaching authority has not yet defined these beliefs as dogmas, much momentum has gathered in the direction of doing so.

This clear trend is of grave concern to Protestants (as well as to some Catholics[1]), as the net effect of these additional doctrines does seriously undermine a biblical, orthodox understanding and expression of the faith (e.g., as affecting the centrality of Christ in salvation). As we proceed in our analysis of the Catholic Mary, the reasons for this will become clear.

Although the belief has never been solemnly proclaimed as dogma, by their ordinary teaching authority the popes have affirmed with ever-increasing vigor that Mary is mother ("in the order of grace") of both the individual believer and the church.

The spiritual motherhood of Mary was first suggested by Origen, then by Epiphanius, Ambrose, and Augustine. In the eighth century, Ambrose Autpert explicitly called Mary the mother of believers and the mother of the nations.[2] "By the thirteenth century, the faithful will be addressing Mary no longer simply as their Lady . . . but as their heavenly mother."[3]

Why is Mary our mother? Pope Leo XIII explained it this way:

> By the very fact that she was chosen to be the Mother of Christ, Our Lord, Who is at the same time our brother, she was singularly endowed above all other mothers with the mission of manifesting and pouring out her mercy upon us. Moreover, if we are indebted to Christ in that He has shared with us in some way the right, peculiarly His own, of calling God our Father and possessing him as such, to Christ's loving generosity we are similarly indebted for sharing in His right to call Mary Mother and to possess her as such. Just as the most holy Virgin is the Mother (*Genetrix*) of Jesus Christ, so she is the Mother of all Christians, whom indeed she bore (*generavit*) on Mt. Calvary amid the supreme throes of the Redeemer; also, Jesus Christ is as the first-born of all Christians, who by adoption and Redemption are his brothers.[4]

Pope Pius X added this perspective:

> For is not Mary the Mother of Christ? She is therefore our Mother also . . . as the God-Man He acquired a body composed like that of other men, but as the Saviour of our race He had a

From Lowly Handmaid to Queen of Heaven

kind of spiritual and mystical Body, which is the society of those who believe in Christ. . . .

Consequently, Mary, bearing in her womb the Savior, may be said to have borne also all those whose life was contained in the life of the Saviour. All of us, therefore, who are united with Christ and are, as the Apostle says, "Members of his body, made from his flesh and from His bones" (Eph. 5:30), have come forth from the womb of Mary as a body united to its head. Hence, in a spiritual and mystical sense, we are called children of Mary, and she is the Mother of us all . . . the Most Blessed Virgin is at once the Mother of God and of man.[5]

The function of Mary as spiritual mother was described by Pope Benedict XV:

She, having been constituted by Jesus Christ as the Mother of all men, received them as bequeathed to her by a testament of infinite charity, and since with maternal tenderness she fulfills her office of protecting their spiritual life, the Sorrowful Virgin cannot but assist, more zealously than ever, her most dear sons by adoption at that moment when their eternal salvation is at stake.[6]

As is so often the case with Catholic Mariology, the scriptural support for this doctrine is weak in the extreme. To the Protestant, who views Scripture as the only secure anchor for theology, Catholic Mariology having cut loose from this anchor is hopelessly adrift upon a sea of splendid but dubious "Roman logic." As Victor Buksbazen puts it: "The non-Catholic student of Mariology who tries to follow its shaky premises and strained conclusions finds himself in a kind of theological *Alice in Wonderland* in which things, in spite of their seeming logic, become 'curiouser and curiouser.'"[7]

The primary proof text for Mary's spiritual motherhood is John 19:25–27, from which we are supposed to gather that Jesus entrusted all men into Mary's maternal care: "Seeing his mother there with the disciple whom he loved, Jesus said to his mother, 'Woman, there is your son.' In turn he said to the disciple, 'There is your mother.' From that hour onward, the disciple took her into his care."

O'Carroll admits: "The Fathers of the Church and early Christian writers did not so interpret the words of the dying Christ. Development of the idea of Mary's spiritual motherhood was slow and did not enter the consciousness of the Church until medieval times. During those early centuries, the sacred text did not immediately convey the notion. Lengthy reflection was needed to reach it."[8]

Frank Sheed presents perhaps the best example of this "lengthy reflection" (the above Scripture passage has been used as a proof text in conflicting ways):

> The appointment [of Mary as our spiritual mother] was made upon Calvary. When Our Lord gave her the Apostle John to be her son, he was not simply making provision for her. For that he had no need to wait for Calvary; he could have attended to it before his crucifixion and after his Resurrection. Calvary was the sacrifice of the race's redemption; everything that he did and said on the cross related to that. So with his word to Our Lady and St. John. It was as part of his plan of redemption, that he was giving her to be the mother of John—not of John as himself but as man. From this moment she is the mother of us all.[9]

Protestants contend that only a predisposed ambition to produce a "spiritual mother" could lead to such a reading of this text. That Jesus had only John, and not all men and women, in mind is made sufficiently clear by John's comment that from that day on *he* took Mary into *his* care. If the fact that Mary was now to look on John as her son means that she was also to look on all believers as her children, then the fact that Mary was simultaneously entrusted to John's care would have to mean that she was also entrusted to the care of all believers, which is absurd.

Although Sheed's argument that everything Jesus said on the cross had to have redemptive significance may at first seem plausible, there is no biblical basis for saying it must be so. Rather, the account fits in well with one of the apostle John's literary objectives: to provide intimate insights into the warm care Jesus demonstrated toward his loved ones (see John 13:22–30; 20:11–18; and all of chapter 21). Jesus, seeing his mother and his "beloved disciple" together at the foot of the cross, demonstrated once again the selfless love he would have us emulate—his taking care of the needs of his mother despite the unthinkable agony he was enduring.

Apart from lack of scriptural proof texts, the Catholic theological reasoning used to explain this doctrine does not follow. True, our life is contained in the life of the Son, and Mary is his mother, but this does not make her our mother in any way. The new birth we have in Jesus Christ is spiritual in nature (John 3:3–8). The birth that Jesus had through Mary was according to the flesh. Jesus derived his physical life through Mary, but that is not what he came to communicate to us. He derived his spiritual life from the Father, and we derive our spiritual life from him. As Jesus said: "It is the Spirit who gives life; the flesh profits nothing; the words that I have spoken to you are spirit and are life" (John 6:63). To sum up, we receive life from Christ on a plane that relates back to the Father, not on a plane that relates back to Mary; hence, Mary is not our mother.

6

Coredemptrix and Mediatrix

Mary's title of spiritual mother provides a context for additional titles the church has assigned to her: coredemptrix and mediatrix, or coredemptress and mediatress—the feminine forms of coredeemer and mediator. Mediatrix is sometimes used inclusively for both functions; it also includes within its scope yet another title: dispensatrix of all graces. In the words of Ludwig Ott: "As Mary became the spiritual Mother of all the redeemed, it is fitting that she by her constant motherly intercession should care for the supernatural life of all her children."[1]

Such warm maternal imagery notwithstanding, to the majority of Protestants these are (for reasons we shall soon see) among the most objectionable of all Catholic beliefs concerning Mary. Karl Keating concedes: "As a practical matter, this kind of doctrine is one of the last accepted by someone approaching the Church, particularly someone coming to the Church from fundamentalism, and it is accepted, ultimately, on the authority of the Church rather than on the authority of clear scriptural references."[2]

Mariologists see two distinct aspects to Mary's work on our behalf: objective redemption (associated with her role as coredemptrix) and subjective redemption (associated with her role as mediatrix). Objective redemption refers to Mary's part in the sacrificial offering of Christ for the sins of humanity. Mary is seen as coredemptrix at the least in her assent to be the mother of the Savior of the world. As we shall see in more detail shortly, many Catholic theologians take the theme far beyond this. Subjective redemption refers to Mary's cooperation with Christ in the application of his redemptive grace to mankind.

Coredemptrix

The role of Mary in the work of redemption is the foremost area of Mariological inquiry today. The discussion has not been without controversy among Catholics. Over the past few decades two opposing camps—the "minimalists" and the "maximalists"—have ardently sought to bring the church into alignment with their own convictions. The more ecumenically minded minimalists hold that Mary's place in Catholic spirituality should be "kept in proportion" to the central place of Christ. The maximalists, who tend to be stout traditionalists, wish to see Mary's mediating function strongly emphasized. They contend that all of the defined Marian dogmas (which the minimalists do accept) naturally culminate in the belief that Mary is *actively* involved in man's salvation. They have called on the papacy to define this belief as dogma.

Although the doctrine has yet to be defined (it is commonly believed to be the next one in line), in official documents many popes have avidly propounded what amounts to a maximalist view.

The seeds of this belief were planted as early as the second century. Irenaeus, picking up on an idea that had previously been promoted by Justin Martyr, wrote: "Eve disobedient became the cause of death for herself and all the human race. Mary obedient became the cause of salvation for herself and the human race."[3] (It is probably safe to say that the contrasting of Mary with Eve, which began in the mid-second century, was the actual beginning of what has gradually developed into today's Catholic Mariology.) By the time of Jerome (late fourth, early fifth centuries), "Death by Eve, life by Mary" was almost a proverb. This trend was greatly propelled by Jerome's *Vulgate* (a translation of the Bible into Latin), which erroneously rendered a pronoun in Genesis 3:15 in the feminine gender, saying a woman will bruise the serpent's head.

The title coredemptrix has been in use since the fifteenth century, and was first officially sanctioned by the papacy when Pius X ascribed it to Mary in 1908.

Catholic theology understands Mary's role in redemption to be directly related to her status as the mother of God. Pius XI stated: "The most blessed Virgin, conceived without original sin, was chosen to be the Mother of God so that she might be made an associate in the Redemption of mankind."[4]

Mediatrix

In practice, the church has looked to Mary as mediatrix and dispensatrix of all graces since medieval times. It became common to refer to Mary as the "neck" within Christ's mystical body, through which everything that comes to us from the head (Christ) must pass, and through which also we must pass in order to reach the head. The church maintains that in keeping with Mary's role as dispensatrix of all graces, no grace is received by man that does not come through Mary.

Recognizing the controversial nature of such teachings, church theologians have been careful to clarify that it was Christ alone who successfully atoned for our sins and bought redemption for us all, including Mary. Her intercession is not intrinsically necessary. However, it is the Father's good pleasure that none of Christ's graces be conferred on us without the intercession of his mother. In theory these theologians state that "coredemption is still only a subordinate, secondary, dependent collaboration in Christ's all-perfect, self-sufficient work of salvation."[5] However, despite these efforts to protect the all-important, orthodox doctrine of the atonement, all of the emphasis that has been placed on Mary's mediation by the popes on down virtually assured that in practice the Catholic faithful would often look more to Mary for grace than to her Son.

Modern Popes Clarify Mary's Role

To illustrate this point, and to get a better understanding of exactly what the church refers to when it speaks of objective redemption and subjective redemption, let us consider the following quotations of modern popes on both subjects. Pius X in *Ad Diem Illum* contributed significantly to twentieth-century thought on Mary as coredemptrix:

> The most holy Mother of God had not only the honor of "having given the substance of her flesh to the only begotten Son of God, who was to be born of the human race," and by means of this flesh the Victim for the salvation of man was to be prepared, but she was also entrusted with the task of tending and nourishing this Victim and even of offering it on the altar at the appointed time.[6]

Benedict XV further elaborated the role Mary played:

> Thus, she (Mary) suffered and all but died along with her Son suffering and dying; thus, for the salvation of men she abdicated the rights of a mother toward her Son, and insofar as was hers to do, she immolated the Son to placate God's justice, so that she herself may justly be said to have redeemed together with Christ the human race.[7]

Mary's function as mediatrix is explained by Leo XIII in *Magnae Dei Matris*:

When we have recourse to Mary in prayer, we are having recourse to the Mother of mercy, who is so well disposed toward us that, whatever the necessity that presses upon us, especially in attaining eternal life, she is instantly at our side of her own accord, even though she has not been invoked; and dispenses grace with a generous hand from that treasure with which from the beginning she was divinely endowed in fullest abundance that she might be worthy to be the Mother of God.[8]

The same pope stresses that Mary's status as mediatrix is both central and universal:

Nothing whatever of that immense treasure of all graces, which the Lord brought us . . . is granted to us save through Mary, so that, just as no one can come to the Father on high except through the Son, so almost in the same manner, no one can come to Christ except through his Mother.[9]

Implicit or Imagined?

Mariologists hold that Mary's role in redemption is implicit in Scripture. As previously indicated, strong emphasis is placed on Luke 1:38, where Mary responds to her divine calling to be the mother of the Savior: "I am the servant of the Lord. Let it be done to me as you say." Ott's interpretation of this verse is typical: "The Incarnation of the Son of God, and the Redemption of mankind by the vicarious atonement of Christ were dependent on her assent."[10]

Nowhere does the Bible teach such an inflated concept of Mary's role, as though the fate of all humanity were hanging on her choice. God determined before time began that he would redeem the world through the death of his Son (1 Pet. 1:20–21), and all that has happened in history concerning the atonement was merely the outworking of his predetermined will. No human being could have

From Lowly Handmaid to Queen of Heaven

stood in the way of this; to hold otherwise would mean to deny the central biblical doctrine of God's sovereignty (see Ps. 115:3).

As G. C. Berkouwer reports it, Catholic minimalists have brought out several problems with the maximalist view of Mary's cooperation in redemption, including the following: They ask "how Mary could be co-redemptrix in gaining the salvation that she herself needed." They argue that if salvation is dependent on Mary's "fiat" (her assent to give birth to the Redeemer), then "redemption stems from two components—the act of God in Christ and the act of Mary." Furthermore, they ask, "Since Mary remains human, would not her status as co-redemptrix mean that salvation has an earthly source?"[11] All of these questions pose serious theological problems, even for Catholic theology, and the maximalists have not resolved them.

In defense of Mary as dispensatrix of all graces, Ott presents the following argument: "Since Mary gave the source of all grace to men, it is to be expected that she would also co-operate in the distribution of all grace."[12] Again we find an unduly inflated view of Mary's role. One would gather from such an assertion that the eternal Logos—the second person of the Holy Trinity—was Mary's to give.

Without wishing to detract from her rightful honor, it must be stated that Mary's part in the incarnation was merely as the vehicle chosen by the Triune God for the Logos's entry into this world. After this she was also called to provide maternal care for the divine child. In Scripture, after these functions are accomplished she recedes into the background and we read little of her. (In this sense she has rightly been compared with John the Baptist, who, after he accomplished *his* preparatory purpose, said: "He must increase while I must decrease" [John 2:30].) Nowhere in the epistles is her role in the dispensing of graces mentioned, while the Holy Spirit's function in the same capacity is clearly taught.[13] Therefore, Ott's reasoning cannot be substantiated.

The One and Only Mediator:
The Protestant Response

The central problem with the doctrine of Mary as mediatrix—indeed, the most critical problem in all of Catholic Mariology—is its clear violation of 1 Timothy 2:5: "There is one God, and one mediator also between God and men, the man Christ Jesus" (NASB). If this were an isolated passage in Scripture, perhaps it would be easier to discard. However, this verse simply summarizes a major theme of the entire New Testament, especially the Epistle to the Hebrews.

Christ is seen in Hebrews as the sole and entirely sufficient agent in effecting our redemption from beginning to end. He alone was worthy to serve as a sacrifice for our sins (9:12–14; 10:1–10). As our great high priest, only he could offer this sacrifice of himself (9:14, 25–26; 10:11–12). Having perfectly satisfied man's debt of sin before God (10:10–18), he now sits as our high priest and advocate at the right hand of God (8:1; 9:24; 10:12). On the basis of his complete identification with man and full participation in the human experience, he perfectly sympathizes with our plight and continually makes intercession for us (2:16–18; 4:14–15; 7:25). Because of the superiority and permanence of his high priestly work, all other mediators have been set aside (7:23–28; 8:6, 13). We obtain confident access to the very throne of God through him, receiving all of the grace and mercy we need (2:18; 4:16; 10:19–22); thus there is no need for any other's mediation.

All of these truths stand behind Paul's simple declaration that "there is one mediator between God and men." Only by violating them can the church teach that Mary is coredemptrix and mediatrix.

In response to this charge, maximalists attempt to show that they do not truly contradict such biblical passages. Michael O'Carroll is a case in point:

From Lowly Handmaid to Queen of Heaven

The use of "one" (*eis* not *monos*) emphasizes Christ's transcendence as a mediator, through the unique value of his redemptive death. The context is the salvation of the infidel, as the following verse makes clear: "God, our Saviour, desires all men to be saved and to come to the knowledge of the truth." This is a statement of the universality of salvation, not of Christ's relationship towards those who have already come to him.[14]

I must first of all point out that the apostle Paul's use of the Greek word *eis* instead of *monos* for "one" in no way weakens the idea that Christ is the only mediator. According to *Thayer's Greek-English Lexicon of the New Testament*, the second major usage of *eis* is emphatic, "so that others are excluded," and 1 Timothy 2:5 is cited as an example of this. Included among other instances of *eis* being used emphatically rather than universally (too numerous to list *in toto*) are the following particularly pertinent examples: James 4:12; Matthew 19:17; 23:8–9; Mark 12:32; John 7:21; 11:50; 1 Corinthians 8:4, 6; 9:24; 2 Corinthians 5:14; Galatians 3:20; 1 Timothy 3:2, 12.

O'Carroll sets up a false distinction between *eis* and *monos* to try to convince us that Paul does not exclude other mediators. The fact is that Paul could not have used *monos* in this case without changing the structure and sense of his sentence. *Monos* means "only" or "alone" and is never used to signify an ordinal (the number one). But that is clearly what Paul wanted to signify: There is (only) one God and (only) one mediator.

Paul's reference to there being "one God" in immediate relationship to there being "one mediator" creates further problems for O'Carroll's position. Did Paul only mean to imply that the biblical God is transcendent over other gods; that there could be other gods, as long as they were subordinate to him? Certainly this is not a Catholic view. And yet, the word *one* is used in the same sense for Christ as mediator as it is for Yahweh as God. Therefore, the text does not allow for the idea of a subordinate mediator to Christ such as Mary.

O'Carroll is right that, in context, Paul is speaking of the infidel and not those who have already come to Christ. But in any case the natural sense of the affirmation that "there is one mediator between God and men" is absolute and unconditional: he is the only mediator at all points in the salvation process, both before faith and after. Furthermore, to say that Paul is speaking only of the infidel does not eliminate the Catholic dilemma: the verse would still refute the doctrine that Mary participated in the salvation of humanity as coredemptrix.

Another approach to justify Mary's mediation, demonstrated in the following quotation by Sheed, is to argue that, in a sense, *all* believers are called to be mediators:

> St. Pius X called her "the first steward in the dispensing of all graces." With this we come to an element in the Redemption which we too easily fail to notice. Christ redeemed us, but it is in God's plan that the application to individual souls of the redemption Christ won should be by fellow members of the race . . . we are all called to be stewards in the dispensing of graces. . . . St. Paul can tell his converts to pray for others *precisely because* there is one Mediator between God and man (1 Tim. 2:5). In other words, the fact that our Lord is Mediator does not make our prayer for one another unnecessary; it makes it effective. Everyone's prayers can help others, but the holier, the more. . . . All are meant to take a part in his redeeming work, but Mary above all.[15]

Sheed here displays why he is among the foremost Catholic apologists: his argument has a disarming effect, because there is a strong element of truth in it. Believers *are* called to participate subordinately in Christ's mediating work (e.g., 1 Pet. 2:9; 2 Cor. 5:20). However, this is not the issue. As Catholics will agree, while others besides Christ can play mediating roles between men and God, there is a line of demarcation that separates the mediation of Christ from that of all others: certain critical attributes and functions that only he can possess and perform. And it is the Protestant contention that, in certain significant respects, Catholicism places Mary on Christ's side of that line.

One all-important example is the central priestly function of making expiation for sin. Now, as we've already seen, the church would theoretically agree that this is something Christ alone can do; and it should be acknowledged that in the early twentieth century the papacy condemned an effort to assign the title "priest" to Mary. Nonetheless, the doctrine that Mary was an associate in the atonement seriously undermines this biblical stand.

As mediators, believers can represent God to man (through proclaiming his Word) and man to God (through prayer). But, as we shall see more clearly in chapter 9, no departed believer is shown in Scripture to be the *object* of prayer. Biblically, a person who prays talks to God through the mediation of the God-man, Jesus Christ. No heavenly entities other than the persons of the Trinity figure into the picture. Humanity's link to heaven is "limited" to the unlimited: God. Why should we need anything else? This is the significance of the incarnation: because he is man, Christ is able to function as our mediator; because he is God, we have direct access into the presence of deity and never have to settle for anything less. Therefore, linking Mary in the heavenly chain between Jesus and man not only places Mary in a mediating position unoccupied by other believers, it depreciates the all-sufficiency and glory of Christ's priesthood.

Furthermore, the church portrays the basis for Mary's mediation as being more like that of Christ than that of believers. Christ is qualified to serve as mediator between man and God because of his absolute holiness (see Heb. 7:26). Believers, on the other hand, all are qualified to pray, for themselves or others, strictly on the basis of Christ's imputed merits, received through faith (Rom. 3:21–28; Eph. 3:12). While some may be more *effective* in prayer because of the moral character of their lives (see James 5:16), they all stand on the same ground, which has nothing to do with their own personal holiness. But the Catholic Mary supposedly serves as mediatrix on the basis of her perfect holiness—the same basis that Christ serves on. Sheed alludes to this in the above quotation. Pope John Paul II makes it clearer still: "In Mary's case we have a special and exceptional mediation, based upon her 'fullness of grace,' [sinlessness]."[16] Even if we grant that this holiness is the "imparted righteousness of Christ," as the church teaches, it is still in a real sense hers. This places her in a similar light as Christ, again diluting the uniqueness of his priestly role.[17]

The church appears to have painted itself into a theological corner. In trying not to detract from Christ, its theologians have so defined the role of Mary as to make it entirely dispensable: everything we need we get from Christ. If that's the case, what is the point or importance of Mary's mediation?

On the other hand, the oft-heard affirmation that Mary can influence her Son to help us necessarily implies that the Son otherwise would be less disposed to do so. In fact, the very concept of a mediator presupposes that there are differences that need to be reconciled between two parties. This leads to the inescapable conclusion that, apart from Mary's mediation, Christ himself would not be perfectly reconciled to us. All this seriously compromises the integrity of his high priesthood.

The church is stuck in a hopeless dilemma wherein either Mary's role is rendered superfluous, or the all-sufficiency of Christ's mediation is diminished. In trying to avoid either of these perceived pitfalls, it has fallen headlong into both.

Mary as Mediatrix in Devotional Literature

While official Catholic theological formulations are often carefully worded in an (ultimately unsuccessful) effort to protect Christ's mediation, devotional interpretations unambiguously fail to do so. These usually receive sanction and not censure from the church (herein the hierarchy's culpability is particularly evident). Among the all-too-accessible examples that could be cited, consider the following excerpts (chosen because they are representative of the genre, not because they are outstandingly bad) from *Novena Prayers in Honor of Our Mother of Perpetual Help*, a booklet published by the Sisters of St. Basil with official church approval (*Nihil Obstat* and *Imprimatur*):[18]

> Have pity, compassionate Mother, on us and our families; especially in this my necessity (here mention it). Help me, O my Mother, in my distress; deliver me from all my ills; or if it be the will of God that I should suffer still longer, grant that I may endure all with love and patience. This grace I expect of thee with confidence, because thou art our Perpetual Help (p. 5).

> We have no greater help,
> no greater hope than you,
> O Most Pure Virgin; help us, then,
> for we hope in you, we glory in you,
> we are your servants.
> Do not disappoint us (p. 16).

> Come to my aid, dearest Mother, for I recommend myself to thee. In thy hands I place my eternal salvation, and to thee I entrust my soul. Count me among thy most devoted servants; take me under thy protection, and it is enough for me. For, if thou protect me, dear Mother, I fear nothing; not from my sins, because thou wilt obtain for me the pardon of them; nor from the devils, because thou art more powerful than all hell together; not even from Jesus, my Judge, because by one prayer from thee, He will be appeased. But one thing I fear, that in the hour of temptation, I may through negligence fail to have recourse to thee and thus perish miserably. Obtain for me, therefore, the pardon of my sins, love for Jesus, final perseverance, and the grace to have recourse to thee, O Mother of Perpetual Help (p. 19).

Certainly, these prayers reveal a piety that must be respected, at least for its sincerity. But they also illuminate the fact that the church's inadequate view of Christ's mediation is directly related to its doctrine of justification.

Can Our Advocate Also Be Our Judge?

Catholicism teaches that good works are a *cause* of salvation, while the Protestant Reformation maintained that they are a necessary *result* of it. In the Protestant view, salvation is assured to the true believer because it has been *received* as a *gift* by grace through faith (Eph. 2:8–9; Rom. 3:21–24). Thus, since the Christian is already saved, Christ no longer relates to him or her as judge (i.e., respecting salvation: John 3:16–18; 5:24). But for Catholics, who have no assurance that their future works will be good, it is generally considered presumptuous to say one is saved; therefore, the very real possibility of a Christian falling into eternal damnation poses a constant danger (as can be seen in the third prayer above). And so, Christ can be viewed either as advocate or judge *by the same person.*

On the other hand, Catholics see Mary as pure advocate, since she is the "mother of mercy" and is not responsible for the retribution of sin. This helps explain the extremely lamentable (though not at all uncommon, as we shall see below) assertion that because of Mary's intercession the penitent has nothing to fear from Jesus the judge. Certainly this notion flies in the face of Hebrews 4:15–16. It also makes hollow the church's assurance that Mary's mediation "neither takes away anything from nor adds anything to the dignity and efficacy of Christ the one Mediator."[19]

We might further note the following from the above prayers: (1) They are not just a case of "asking a fellow-Christian to pray for you," as prayer to Mary is so often portrayed. Mary is viewed as actively performing redemptive and mediatorial functions that Scripture exclusively ascribes to Jesus, again pointing up the fact that Mary's role in salvation is understood to be much more like

From Lowly Handmaid to Queen of Heaven

Christ's than that of all other believers. A Christian would hardly entrust his or her soul and eternal salvation into the hands of a mere fellow-believer. Belief in Mary as coredemptrix, therefore, cannot be justified by the fact that Christians also play (through preaching, prayer, etc.) a role in leading souls to salvation.

(2) The absolute and total adoration and trust that belong only to deity are lavished on Mary. The claim that prayer to Mary actually honors Christ's mediation is rendered quite unbelievable when the church approves affirmations such as "We have no greater help, no greater hope" than Mary. How easily the belief that she always receives what she asks of her Son devolves into a belief in her virtual omnipotence!

The "Glories of Mary"

It has been my intention throughout this study to fairly represent the theology of Roman Catholicism. At many points I could have used quotations more appalling to Protestant sensibilities, but I do not desire to present radical Marian devotion as being that of the mainstream church. However, if we totally ignore the extremists we will not clearly see the abuses that mainstream Catholic Mariology inevitably leads to. It will be enlightening for us to turn our attention to how the role of Mary as mediatrix was developed by Alphonsus de Liguori.

Actually, although some of Liguori's comments (and those he presents from numerous saints and respected devotional writers) are extreme compared with official statements of the church, he was by no means on the fringe of Catholicism. He is a canonized saint, was a renowned bishop, and his *The Glories of Mary* (in which the following quotations appear), published in 1750, has been the most celebrated Marian devotional work in the Catholic church—over 800 editions in many languages. To the millions of Catholics who participate in the cult of the Virgin, Liguori's book is not extreme at all. Let us, therefore, examine the extent to which

Liguori and others have exalted Mary at the expense of Jesus, with the approval of the church:

> With reason does an ancient writer call her "the only hope of sinners"; for by her help alone can we hope for the remission of sins.[20]

> He fails and is lost who has not recourse to Mary.[21]

> Shall we scruple to ask her to save us, when "the way of salvation is open to none otherwise than through Mary"?[22]

> [St. Peter Damian] addresses her in these words: "All power is given to thee in Heaven and on earth, and nothing is impossible to thee who canst raise those who are in despair to the hope of salvation."

> "At the command of Mary all obey—even God." St. Bernardine fears not to utter this sentence; meaning, indeed, to say that God grants the prayers of Mary as if they were commands. . . . Since the Mother, then, should have the same power as the Son, rightly has Jesus, who is omnipotent, made Mary also omnipotent; though, of course, it is always true that where the Son is omnipotent by nature, the Mother is only so by grace."[23]

> "There is no doubt," [St. Bernard] adds, "that Jesus Christ is the only mediator of justice between men and God; . . . but because men acknowledge and fear the divine Majesty, which is in him as God, for this reason it was necessary to assign us another advocate, to whom we might have recourse with less fear and more confidence, and this advocate is Mary, than whom we cannot find one more powerful with his divine majesty, or one more merciful towards ourselves. . . . A mediator, then, was needed with the mediator himself."[24]

From Lowly Handmaid to Queen of Heaven

"Be comforted then, O you who fear," will I say with St. Thomas of Villanova: "breathe freely and take courage, O wretched sinners; this great Virgin, who is the Mother of your God and judge, is also the advocate of the whole human race; fit for this office, for she can do what she wills with God; most wise, for she knows all the means of appeasing him; universal, for she welcomes all, and refuses to defend no one."[25]

St. Anselm, to increase our confidence, adds, that "when we have recourse to this divine Mother, not only we may be sure of her protection, but that often we shall be heard more quickly, and be thus preserved, if we have recourse to Mary and call on her holy name, than we should be if we called on the name of Jesus our Saviour," and the reason he gives for it is, "that to Jesus as a judge, it belongs also to punish; but mercy alone belongs to the Blessed Virgin as a patroness."[26]

"Many things," says Nicephorus, "are asked from God, and are not granted; they are asked from Mary, and are obtained."[27]

If God is angry with a sinner, and Mary takes him under her protection, she withholds the avenging arm of her Son, and saves him.[28]

[Prayer of St. Ephram:] O Immaculate Virgin, we are under thy protection . . . we beseech thee to prevent thy beloved Son, who is irritated by our sins, from abandoning us to the power of the devil.[29]

In Liguori and the writers he quotes we come disturbingly close to the fulfillment of a discernible trend that began many centuries ago: the virtual usurping of Christ from the unique position Scripture gives him in order to replace him—for all intents and purposes—with his mother after the flesh. Historically within the church there has existed an urge, usually unconscious, to exalt Mary at almost any cost. Because of the church's original sensitivity to the centrality of Christ,[30] this desire could only find its fulfillment through an age-long altering of Mary: the gradual metamorphosis of the lowly handmaid Scripture portrays into the exalted queen of heaven we are here considering. One shudders to imagine the revulsion the true "bondslave of the Lord" (Luke 1:38, NASB) would feel, knowing such idolatrous adoration has been heaped on her.

It is the Protestant hope that the church will recognize that this entire trend has been unbiblical and thus renounce it. If, because it would involve accepting that they are in fact fallible, the hierarchy refuses to consider this option, then we can only hope that they will carry the process no further, that the position of the minimalists will prevail, and that the church will not define the doctrines of Mary as coredemptrix and mediatrix as Catholic dogma.

There is much overlap between belief in Mary's mediation and the Catholic practice of venerating her. We will, therefore, have more to consider about Mary's role as mediatrix in chapter 8.

From Lowly Handmaid to Queen of Heaven

7

Queen of Heaven

As we turn to the final Marian title that we shall consider in this analysis, the picture of Mary's exaltation begins to look complete. Pius X portrays the Catholic view: "Christ 'has taken His seat at the right hand of the Majesty on high' . . . and Mary as Queen stands at His right hand."[1]

Once again we see how each doctrine exalting Mary has given rise to another. The rationale supplied for her queenship is explained by Ott:

Mary's right to reign as Queen of Heaven is a consequence of her Divine Motherhood. . . . Furthermore, Mary's royal merit is based on her intrinsic connection with Christ in His work of Redemption. Just as Christ is also our Lord and King because He has redeemed us with His precious Blood . . . so, in an analogical way, Mary is Our Lady and Queen because she the new Eve has shared intimately in the redemptive work of Christ, the new

Adam, by suffering with Him and offering Him up to the Eternal Father.[2]

Pius XII, a strong advocate of Mary's queenship, adds this perspective:

He, the Son of God, reflects on His heavenly Mother the glory, the majesty and the dominion of His kingship, for having been associated to the King of Martyrs in the ineffable work of human Redemption as Mother and co-operatrix, she remains forever associated to Him, with an almost unlimited power, in the distribution of the graces which flow from the Redemption. Jesus is King throughout all eternity by nature and by right of conquest; through Him, with Him and subordinate to Him, Mary is Queen by grace, by divine relationship, by right of conquest and by singular election. And her kingdom is as vast as that of her son and God, since nothing is excluded from her dominion. And this queenship of hers is essentially maternal, exclusively beneficent.[3]

The title Queen was first used for Mary by Pope Martin in the seventh century. Boniface IX (1389–1404) called her Perfect Queen, royal Virgin, Queen of the heavens.[4] Sixtus IV in the following century acknowledged her as Queen of heaven. It was only a matter of time before Mary would be supplicated by Catholics around the world as queen of heaven, queen of the angels, queen of demons, queen of patriarchs, queen of prophets, queen of apostles, queen of martyrs, queen of virgins, queen of confessors, and queen of saints.

The pattern we've observed in which the church has gradually exalted Mary to the position of queen of heaven is typical of religious traditions throughout the world. Although when alive they often denounced such efforts, in the centuries that succeeded their deaths key figures in the origins of major religions have been raised by the faithful to various levels of quasideity. The actual facts of

From Lowly Handmaid to Queen of Heaven

these figures' lives would then become blurred by legends. Majestic titles would be assigned to them. They would be honored with important roles in the salvation of mankind. Whether it was the legend of Muhammad's ascent into heaven, the exalting of Guatama Buddha (whom many scholars consider an atheist) to the position of eternal deity, or the extreme veneration of the pragmatic Confucius, the tendency has been consistent. We may contend that such inclinations are ingrained in the religious nature of "natural man" (1 Cor. 2:14).

It should not be surprising to find that over a two-thousand-year period such a near-universal pattern has found expression in Christianity. Although Christianity is based in divine revelation, in its social dimension it unavoidably accumulates trappings common to a world religion. Thus people have imposed their ways on divine revelation, and the exaltation of Mary has been one of the many results.[5]

Another factor that contributed to the exaltation of Mary was that there existed in the Greco-Roman culture, as a result of their age-long obsession with mythological gods and goddesses, a predisposed yearning for a mother-queen goddess figure. Now, it must be acknowledged that much of what has been written along these lines has been overly polemical, with dubious scholarship. However, this does not necessarily nullify the argument; it does mean that greater care needs to be taken in the presenting of it. I believe Buksbazen has fairly and accurately summarized the facts:

> The ancient world of the Semitic, Egyptian, Greek and Roman civilizations abounded in gods and goddesses which personified the forces of fertility, of spring and awakening new life. To the Semitic peoples the goddess of fertility was known as Ishtar or Astarte; the Egyptians worshipped her as Isis, the spouse of Osiris; the Greeks worshipped her as Athena, Demeter, Cybele or Diana. To the Romans she was known as Juno or Minerva. To all of them she was familiar as the Great Mother or Queen of

Heaven. Even the Israelites, in spite of their strong monotheistic heritage, succumbed to this all-pervading and insidious cult, apparently brought by them from Egypt. This cult was especially popular among the women (Jeremiah 44:17, 25). [Note: the title *Queen of Heaven* itself is used of the goddess in this and other passages in Jeremiah.] If this cult was able to exert such a potent influence on monotheistic Jews, how much more pervasive must its impact have been upon the newly-baptized and only superficially converted pagans?

When Christianity spread throughout the Roman Empire around the shores of the Mediterranean, the forces of paganism were still very strong. Under this influence a gradual and subtle transformation took place, whereby Mary replaced the old goddesses in the devotion of the new converts. At the same time, shrines dedicated to Mary began to replace the ancient temples of her former pagan rivals. The old saying, *victi, victoribus leges diderunt*—"The conquered impose their laws (or, as in this case their cults) on the conquerors," was certainly true in this situation.

Although Christianity was superficially victorious, paganism remained deep-rooted and would not surrender without a stubborn and protracted battle. In fact, paganism never fully surrendered to Christianity. Imperceptibly and subtly, it survived and strongly influenced the early church, its institutions, its doctrines and its mode of worship. Although the tree of paganism was cut down, the roots remained deep in the soil and helped transform Miriam of the Gospel into Mary of Popular piety—later into Mariological dogma.[6]

In response to such claims, Karl Keating rejoins: "One of the problems with this argument is timing. Paganism effectively disappeared by the end of the sixth century, but devotion to Mary of a sort seen today was not common until the Middle Ages, by which time paganism was not even a distant memory."[7]

It is true that the cult of Mary did not fully flower until the Middle Ages; one of the points made throughout this work has been that Catholic Mariology has developed very gradually. However, as I indicated in chapter 1, radical devotion to Mary did exist on the fringes of Christianity since around the fourth century.[8] This can be traced directly back to paganism, as virtually all respected Protestant and secular historians attest.[9]

After the leaders of the church declared Mary to be the mother of God, such devotion became more and more acceptable. Thus, it was never really necessary for the (often only) nominally converted subjects of Rome to repent of their longing for a goddess figure; they could just transfer their devotion to the most likely replacement within a Christian context. Such longing was constrained for a time by the Christ-centeredness of the early church, but it nonetheless remained an active part of the Greco-Roman consciousness. As the driving force behind the cult of the Virgin this longing gradually reasserted itself, until by the time of the Middle Ages it had totally permeated and entrenched itself within the church.

In this light it becomes clear that the root of Marian devotion sprang from pagan soil, even if by the time it reached maturity nobody considered themselves pagan.

8

Hyperveneration*

The Protestant must acknowledge that if the practice of venerating Mary could be established from Scripture, then the question of its origins (i.e., pagan influence) would be rendered irrelevant. Ott attempts to rise to the challenge:

> The Scriptural source of the special veneration due to the Mother of God is to be found in Luke 1, 28: "Hail, full of grace, the Lord is with thee," in the praise of Elizabeth, filled with the Holy Ghost, Luke 1, 42: "Blessed art thou amongst women, and blessed is the fruit of thy womb," in the prophetic words of the Mother of God, Luke 1, 48: "For behold, from henceforth, all generations shall call me blessed," in the words of the woman in the multitude, Luke 11, 27: "Blessed is the womb that bore thee, and the paps that gave thee suck."[1]

Although he probably did not mean to be taken this way, the rhetorical effect of Ott's citing the first two passages could easily

---

* A technical term used in Roman Catholic theology.

result in circular reasoning; that is, one could infer that since these exclamations are portions of the *Ave Maria* (or "Hail Mary"), a prayer central to Catholic devotions, they must have been uttered in the scriptural accounts with all the prayerful devotion with which Catholics now recite them. Such reasoning would beg the question, because the fact that Catholics have utilized these words for the purpose of devotional prayer does not prove they were originally uttered in the same spirit. They need only be taken as declarations of fact; meant to convey special honor, to be sure, but not necessarily "special veneration."

On the surface, Mary's proclamation that "all generations shall call me blessed" would seem to sanction the entire history of Marian devotion. However, it does not logically follow that for these words to be prophetic *every* tribute paid to Mary in subsequent generations must be a fulfillment of them. Catholics would agree with Protestants that, though they called Mary blessed, the Collyridians, "a small sect of women who offered cakes to Mary"[2] in the fourth century, did not express the kind of blessing that Mary had in mind. The fact is that Mary has been considered blessed by all generations of Christians, *including* Protestants. Thus, the prophecy has been fulfilled. But nothing in her prophecy rules out the possibility that some (even many) views of and attitudes toward Mary would go beyond biblical bounds; nor does it excuse them when they have in fact done so.

That Luke 11:27 would be cited as a proof text for the veneration of Mary is, from a Protestant perspective, striking evidence of a scriptural blindness where Mary is concerned. To be sure, the woman in the crowd does cry out that Jesus' mother is to be blessed. But what is Jesus' reply? "*Rather*, blest are they who hear the word of God and keep it" (v. 28). It should be obvious that rather than supporting the tendency to venerate Mary this verse refutes it.

Latria, *Dulia,* and *Hyperdulia*

I have avoided using the term *worship* in regard to Catholic devotion to Mary out of respect for the fact that ever since the Second Council of Nicea (A.D. 787) the Catholic church has officially taught that there are three degrees of devotion to be practiced by Christians. The first is *latria,* or worship, to be given to God alone. The second is *dulia,* or veneration, which may be directed to the saints. The third is *hyperdulia,* or hyperveneration, which among all created beings may be offered to Mary alone. While in theory these categories are intended to prevent idolatrous worship of created beings, in practice they have little effect on the religious feelings of the masses. How could *feelings* be subject to such subtle rational distinctions?

The fact is that Mary is, and for centuries has been, worshiped by millions all over the world, especially in the Latin countries, and the church has done very little to discourage it. During the Second Vatican Council the cardinal archbishop of Santiago de Chile, delivering his address in the name of forty-four Latin American bishops, acknowledged: "In Latin American countries devotion to Our Lady is sometimes too far removed from the proper devotional life of the Church."[3] The bishop of Cuernavaca (Mexico) agreed: "Devotion to Mary and the saints, especially in our [Latin American] countries, at times obscures devotion to Christ."[4]

To the Protestant it is clear that the problem of excessive devotion to Mary in Latin countries and elsewhere in the Catholic world is not a case of a legitimate practice gone awry; it is, rather, like the opening of Pandora's box. Once devotion to anyone but God is sanctioned by the hierarchy, there is no way the hierarchy can later constrain it within certain limits. All *sin* operates according to the same "give-it-an-inch-and-it-takes-a-mile" dynamic— and *idolatry* is sin—and *religious devotion* to anyone but God is idolatry. This is the verdict of Scripture.

If one conducts a careful study of the biblical use of the word *prayer*, one finds that it is always used with reference to God, except in a couple of instances where mention is made of the heathen custom of praying to dumb idols. Furthermore, there is no scriptural basis for believing that Mary and the saints would hear prayers uttered to them. And even if they could hear some prayers, Mary could not hear all of the hundreds of thousands of prayers that undoubtedly are addressed to her every minute of the day. As a creature she, by definition, is limited; she cannot be omniscient and omnipresent.

In the Bible we find consistent emphasis on an all-encompassing distinction between God (Father, Son, and Holy Spirit) on the one hand and the entire spectrum of creation (including all angels and human beings) on the other hand. God commands that he alone be worshiped (Luke 4:8; 1 Cor. 1:29). He makes it clear that no created being will glory before him; he will share his glory with no one (Isa. 42:8). Even angels emphatically refuse worship, insisting that all angels and humans are on an equal footing of humility before God (Rev. 22:8–9). In the New Testament we find that even the greatest of the apostles would not stand for being given any of the reverential treatment that is reserved for God alone (Acts 10:25–26; 14:11–15). We must conclude then that biblically all prayer, glory, and devotion belong to God and to his Son, Jesus Christ.

Are Protestants Afraid of Mary?

With characteristic poetic flair, evangelical convert to Catholicism Thomas Howard revolts against such a conclusion:

The Christian piety that has been afraid almost to name, much less to hail, the Virgin and to join the angel Gabriel and Elisabeth in according blessing and exaltation to her is a piety that has impoverished itself. Stalwart for the glory of God alone, it has been afraid to see the amplitude of that glory, which brims and overflows and splashes outward in a surging golden tide, gilding everything that it touches. Saint Francis had an eye for this and exulted in everything made by God. . . . In contrast to this, the punctilious insistence that nothing be exalted and glorified except God alone begins to seem parsimonious.[5]

In light of the biblical survey we just concluded, the Protestant could understandably respond: "What's the use of such sentimental reasoning when the position of Scripture is so clear on the subject? Are you wiser than the apostles, angels, and even God?" But Howard does bring up some points that cannot be so summarily dismissed.

It is true that some Protestants, no doubt in reaction to Catholic excesses, have almost forgotten Mary. But this is no more the will of God than it would be for Christians to ignore Moses, John the Baptist, or the apostles Paul, Peter, and John. In other words, while Mary is not exalted above every other created being in the Bible, she is one of the most important figures to be found in it. "Blessed among women," she is the preeminent feminine model of faith and obedience, worthy of honor and admiration. Just as we can gain much from contemplating and imitating the life and faith of a Paul (1 Cor. 11:1), Elijah, or Samuel, so also from Mary.

Furthermore, there is nothing wrong with recognizing and appreciating the glory of God as it is revealed in creation. And it is also true that in the next creation God's glory will indeed "brim and overflow and splash outward" from his people (1 Cor. 15:43; Phil. 3:21; Col. 3:4).

There are, however, certain limits that must be set so as to keep these truths in biblical perspective. First, we must be careful to direct all praise and adoration for the glory we see in God's creation to him and not to the creature itself (Rom. 1:21–23; Job 31:26–28). Second, there is an infinite gap between admiration on the one hand and veneration on the other, between holding biblical personalities as models to follow and making them the objects of devotional life.

In heaven we will certainly have the opportunity to directly pay these biblical saints the tribute they are due, and to admire the glory that God has given them (as they will likely admire the glory that will be bestowed on us!). But, perhaps because he knows how easily we can fall into idolatry under present conditions, God has not made such contact between us and them possible in the here and now.

Are Catholics Afraid of Christ?

It may be that some Catholics who read this will feel threatened by the suggestion that God would have them abandon their veneration of Mary. Catholics have readily confessed that prayer to Mary, such as the rosary, is a great source of comfort to them. Why is it that so many Catholics feel more comfortable praying to Mary than to Christ?[6]

This brings us back to a discussion of mediation. When (through prayer) we come directly into the presence of God, we become uncomfortably aware of our sins. We fear the divine presence, sensing the need of someone who is fully human like us, someone who understands our weakness and will intercede before God on our behalf. The tragic thing is that so many millions have sought this mediator in a person who, though an exalted servant of God, is neither able nor called to function in that role. It is tragic because there is such a mediator, and he's been available all along (1 Tim. 2:5).

One root of the problem goes back to the manner in which the Christological councils such as Nicea and Chalcedon were interpreted: Christ's deity was emphasized so heavily that the full picture of his humanity was lost sight of. G. C. Berkouwer reports that certain Catholic minimalists agree with this assessment:

The phenomenal appeal of Mary is explained by some [minimalists] in terms of the Church's tendency to dehumanize Christ. P.

Rusch contends that the christological controversies ended by laying such stress on the uniqueness and divinity of Christ that a deep gulf was created between the ordinary believer and his Lord. The distance between Christ and simple piety created a vacuum that was filled by Mary. As Christ the Redeemer disappeared from view, the very human and intimate and religiously appealing figure of Mary drew near to take His place. In the West as well as in the more speculative East, "the mediatorship of Christ declined in the popular religious consciousness," and the image of Mary grew correspondingly large.[7]

Berkouwer summarizes the concern of these minimalists in a way that also summarizes the Protestant concern: "They were convinced that any mediatorial role ascribed to Mary would detract in that proportion from the exclusive mediatorial work of Christ; the very nature of the incarnation was such that an ascription of the work of mediation in any part of [sic] Mary would overshadow the total significance of the fact that the Word did indeed become *man*."[8] We may suggest, then, that a proper understanding of Christ would result in a loss of interest in Mary as an object of faith and devotion.

It is in Christ's *full* humanity (the fact that he is also God makes him no less human than any one of us) that we are able to relate to him and feel comfortable with him. Hebrews 4:15–16, cited earlier, deserves to be printed in full here: "We do not have a high priest who is unable to sympathize with our weakness, but one who was tempted in every way that we are, yet never sinned. So let us confidently approach the throne of grace to receive mercy and favor and to find help in time of need."

The Gender of God

Another factor that has undoubtedly contributed to the historical rise of the cult of the Virgin is the seemingly universal desire for a heavenly mother figure. Since in Scripture God is identified with the masculine pronoun and is represented as our heavenly Father, many feel that they must look elsewhere to find the particular attributes they associate with femininity and motherhood. This very sentiment has also fueled the contemporary rise of goddess-based witchcraft as an alternative to "patriarchal" Christianity.[9]

Whether this desire for a feminine object of religious devotion is legitimate or is an expression of fallen human nature is a question too complicated to address here, except to say that in my view both explanations have some merit. It is therefore necessary to point out that, to the extent that this felt need is legitimate, it can be perfectly satisfied in a relationship with the Father and Christ.

There is much misunderstanding, both in and out of Christian circles, about the "gender" of God. Given the limitations of language, God could only be represented as *he, she,* or *it*. Since God is personal, *it* would not do. Since Adam was created first in God's own image, and Eve was created second out of and for the man (Gen. 2:18, 21–23; 1 Cor. 11:7–9), it was appropriate to identify God by the masculine pronoun rather than the feminine. And it is true that the singularly distinctive manner in which the first person in the Trinity relates to the second (as well as to those of his creatures who adhere to him) is best captured in the word *Father*. Nonetheless, God is infinite Spirit, not an earthbound organism of a particular sex and gender-based orientation.

It is a mistake to think that the characteristics commonly associated with the masculine sex exhaust the attributes of God. A careful look at Genesis 1:27 will show that it is only as male and female that man (the human race) reflects the fullness of God's image. In other words, those desirable qualities found more often in women than men are not in any degree lacking in God; rather (as is also true with the "masculine" attributes found in God), they are raised to infinity and absolute perfection. Thus we find attributed to God such "unmacho" traits as compassion, lovingkindness, graciousness, and tender mercy (Exod. 34:6; Ps. 145:8; Luke 1:78; James 5:11).

Nor should it be thought that because he incarnated as a man, the second person in the Trinity is in short supply of "feminine" virtues. In his earthly life he demonstrated gentleness (2 Cor. 10:1), compassion (Matt. 9:36 is only one of many examples), a freedom to weep openly (John 11:35; Luke 19:41), and a care that can legitimately be called maternal (Luke 13:34).

In other words, any tenderness, compassion, concern, or other expression of care that a Catholic has (vainly, since she's not actually playing such a mediatorial role) looked to Mary to receive can be found fully and freely in the Father and Christ. To hold otherwise, to believe that to adequately meet all of his children's needs God had to elevate one of his female creatures to a level of quasi-deity, is to suggest a deficiency in God's own nature.

In his infinite wisdom our heavenly Father planned our redemption in such a way that we could receive boundless comfort and confidence through the mediation of his Son. If our Catholic brothers and sisters would fully embrace what God has made available to them through their great high priest, they would no longer feel a need for prayer to Mary or any other created being. All of their inner needs will be met in the way God intended—through Jesus.

Part 2

Apparitions of the Virgin Mary: A Protestant Look at a Catholic Phenomenon

Kenneth R. Samples

9

What Is an Apparition?

Devotion to the Blessed Virgin Mary (as she is commonly called by Catholics) has been a centerpiece of Catholic belief and piety for centuries. However, the last century and a half have seen a dramatic increase in Marian devotion. This resurgence of the "cultus of the Virgin" (a reference used by Catholics) can be attributed to two primary factors. First, Mary's already exalted status in the church was substantially enhanced by Catholicism's official acceptance of the Marian dogmas known as the immaculate conception (1854) and the assumption (1950). The second force behind Mary's growth in popularity, especially among the laity, is not so much doctrinal as experiential: her alleged appearances to people throughout the world.

These appearances, called apparitions, have occurred with increasing frequency since the nineteenth century and have attracted widespread attention. Pope Pius XII, in calling attention to the apparitions, referred to the nineteenth century as the "century of Marian predilection [preference]." And the present century cannot be far behind: leading Marian scholar Rene Laurentin notes that there have been more than 200 reported apparitions since the 1930s alone.[1] With the various shrines dedicated to the particular apparitions attracting millions of pilgrims each year, it is easy to see that this phenomenon is having a substantial impact on the almost-one-billion-member Roman Catholic church.

The focus of part 2 of this book will be to address this somewhat mysterious matter of Marian apparitions. In approaching this unusual phenomenon, many questions immediately arise. What actually is an apparition? What were the circumstances surrounding these supposed appearances? How does the Catholic church officially evaluate these claims? And more importantly, at least for evangelicals, what is the biblical perspective on these events? Are they supernatural in origin, or is there some natural or psychological explanation?

The intent, therefore, is to address these questions through a survey of the phenomenon itself (especially its effect on Catholic piety), as well as to furnish a biblical and theological critique. Since this phenomenon is attracting the attention of millions of people throughout the world, it demands careful examination in the light of Scripture.

Surprise Appearances

The word *apparition* comes from the late–Latin word *apparitio* which means "appearance" or "presence." An apparition refers to the sudden appearance of a supernatural entity which directly manifests itself to a human individual or group. Within a Catholic context, it could be the presence or manifestation of any supernatural figure. Catholic scholar Louis Bouyer describes an apparition as "a manifestation of God, angels or the dead (saints or not) appearing under a form that surprises the senses."[2] This revelation to the senses involves sight, but frequently the other senses as well. Some apparitions—usually of Mary—have included the hearing of voices, touching the figure, and the smelling of specific fragrances.

Apparitions, however, are commonly associated with the broader category of religious visions. A respected Catholic dictionary, edited by Donald Attwater, defines an apparition as "the name sometimes reserved for certain kinds of supernatural vision, namely, those that are bodily or visible, as is often used for the manifestation of Our Lady of Lourdes, of St. Michael on Monte Gargano, etc. Owing to the meaning of the word in popular use (ghost, spook), 'appearing' better expresses these events."[3]

While present-day Western psychology frequently equates religious visions with hallucination, Catholicism maintains that an authentic apparition is of a different category. In a hallucination, the content of what is reported is delusionary; it is solely a subjective experience with no correspondence in objective reality.[4] A genuine apparition, on the other hand, is a real subject/object encounter in which the source of the perceived reality is independent of and external to the seer or visionary. One Catholic author describes it this way: "An authentic apparition, therefore, is not a purely subjective experience. It results from a real, 'objective,' intervention of a higher power which enables the beneficiary to make true contact with the being that appears and makes itself known."[5]

The church fully acknowledges that many so-called apparitions can be explained as nothing more than hallucinatory experience. But it maintains that if it can be shown that the seer has experienced a real objective presence that is not of this world, then an authentic apparition has occurred.

Throughout the Middle Ages countless numbers of supposed supernatural manifestations were reported to the church. These included everything from physical healings (often connected to ancient relics) to statues and crucifixes that were reported to have bled. While many of these unusual occurrences have been discredited or rejected in modern times, apparitions have generally remained popular and credible in the eyes of Catholics. People in the past have reported seeing apparitions of Jesus, various saints, and even the devil. But the most enduring and recognizable apparitions are those of the "Blessed Virgin Mary."

Apparitions of Mary

Apparitions of Mary have been reported in church history as early as the fourth century. In fact, while official statistics are not kept, some Catholic theologians have speculated that there have been as many as 21,000 claimed sightings of Mary throughout history.[6] Though this figure may be excessive, the Vatican "has acknowledged a 'surprising increase' in recent years in claims of 'pseudo-mysticism, presumed apparitions, visions and messages' associated with Mary."[7] As stated earlier, Laurentin has counted over two hundred reported apparitions in the past sixty years alone. Another international study produced similar figures and stated that the reports covered thirty-two different countries.[8] In an article discussing Mary's growing popularity, *Insight* magazine stated that "claims of apparitions of Mary are on a worldwide upswing."[9]

10

The Catholic Church's Evaluation

With so many apparitions being reported throughout the world, how does the Catholic church go about evaluating them? The answer is, very cautiously and deliberately. Obviously, the church has much to lose in the area of credibility if it recognizes an apparition which later turns out to be inauthentic or even fraudulent.

As well, this phenomenon is very elusive. How does one go about evaluating a reputedly supernatural manifestation which is, except to the visionaries, invisible? It is safe to say that while the church is open to the possibility of these supernatural manifestations, it is at the same time highly skeptical. In the words of one Catholic scholar: "The church accepts the authenticity of a supernatural intervention only with great circumspection. She requires that the facts, which she submits to a severe examination, should in themselves be striking and also insists on waiting before passing judgment."[1]

According to the Catholic church, apparitions come under the heading of "private revelations." The messages of approved apparitions add nothing to the official (public) revelation of the church, which is found in the apostolic sources of Sacred Scripture and Tradition. While official revelation ended with the apostolic witness, private revelations have continued in the church. Since they contribute no new piece of revelation that is fundamental to the life of the church, apparitions are not binding upon the conscience of individual Catholics. Catholics are free to accept or reject the various apparitions authorized by the church. However, if a Catholic believer is inclined to reject authorized apparitions, he or she should do so with appropriate modesty, guarding against any indulgence in undue criticism.

How the Church Decides

In deciding whether a particular apparition is indeed authentic, the church follows a very deliberate and careful regimen. The process of checking out these unusual events has developed over many centuries of simply struggling with the matter. First of all, if there is sufficient reason to warrant an investigation of a particular claimed apparition, the inquiry begins with the local bishop. He convenes a diocesan commission which is usually made up of various theologians, psychologists, and other trained professionals. Members of the commission attempt to weigh and evaluate the evidence through such means as interviewing and examining the visionaries and testing both the messages and the possible good fruit of the events, such as healings, other miracles, and increased spiritual devotion.

Of paramount importance in evaluating an apparition is to determine whether the message communicated by this supposed supernatural presence is in fact aligned with official church teaching. If anything contained in the apparition is contrary to Catholic teaching, then it is inauthentic and should be rejected. One Catholic source states:

> If the message or messages of an "apparition" are at variance with
> a revealed doctrine or the teaching of the church, that is a clear

Apparitions of the Virgin Mary

sign of nonauthenticity, or conscious or unconscious falsification. It is for ecclesiastical authority (and first of all for bishops in their respective dioceses) to determine if an apparition attributed to Mary meets the guarantees of authenticity. Only then may public veneration in the place of apparition and promulgation of the message be authorized.

The decisions of ecclesial authority in this matter are not infallible and do not command the inner assent of faith. Nevertheless, when the authority "interdicts"—says no—the external compliance demanded of the faithful binds the conscience to obedience. In no way could Mary work against the Church of her Son.[2]

Along with not contradicting official church teaching, apparitions should also not cause division or disunity in the church. Rene Laurentin states that "one of the criteria that a vision comes from God is that it does not divide the church, but remains in charity, order, and obedience."[3] The following five characteristics, Laurentin believes, are exhibited by a genuine apparition, and can thus be used as part of the criteria in evaluating such phenomena: It (1) manifests the hidden presence of God, (2) renews community life, (3) leads to conversion of hearts, (4) promotes the reawakening and stimulation of faith, (5) helps to renew hope and dynamism in the church.[4] These characteristics give some guidelines as to whether a given apparition is bearing genuine fruit.

After the supposed apparition has been carefully scrutinized, the commission votes on whether genuine evidence of the supernatural is connected to it. On completion of the investigation, the bishop makes the commission's findings known to further church officials. The church does not always make an official pronouncement, but when it does it is usually years after the apparition has ceased.

Four Categories of Evaluation

The official evaluations given by the church have generally fallen into four broad categories. These categories were described for me by Catholic scholar Mark Miravalle, assistant professor of theology at the Franciscan University at Steubenville, Ohio, and an authority on Marian apparitions. The first category is those apparitions that are actually "prohibited" by the church. This would include any apparition whose content directly contradicts Catholic faith or morals. Since Catholicism affirms that genuine apparitions would never contradict the official teaching of the church, these apparitions would be considered inauthentic and therefore unworthy of pious belief. The source of this type of apparition could range anywhere from intentional human deception to a manifestation of the demonic.

In the second category the church says nothing officially about a particular apparition. The vast majority of apparitions go unevaluated and unrecognized. Many of these apparitions, while not contrary to Catholic faith and morals, simply lack conclusive evidence to support a supernatural interpretation. Some of these apparitions, however, while not receiving an official evaluation, have received unofficial acceptance, because their shrines are visited by many priests, bishops, and even popes. Such apparitions then are accepted privately by individual Catholics, without receiving an official word from the church.

The third category is somewhat of a neutral class where the church merely states that there is nothing contrary to Catholic faith or morals. In this case the church does not guarantee the authenticity of the apparition but gives its negative approbation or approval. That is, since there is nothing in the messages of these apparitions which runs contrary to church teaching, Catholics are free to incorporate the messages into their lives in accord with the leading of their conscience.

Because apparitions are private revelations, the church does not speak with certainty as to the authenticity of the events. Mark Miravalle explains:

Private revelation consists of a supernatural manifestation of Christian truth made after the close of public revelation (Sacred Scripture and Tradition) with the death of the last apostle. The Church can give her "negative approval" to a private revelation or apparition by stating that there is nothing contained in it that is contrary to faith and morals. In approving an apparition or a revelation, the Church does not intend to guarantee that [sic] authenticity of the respective private revelation, but states that the content of the apparition can be accepted by the faithful without any doctrinal danger in regard to faith and morals.

Yet, it is considered reprehensible if after the Church has given her negative approval of a private revelation, any member of the faithful were to contradict or ridicule the revelation. Further, if after prudent judgment, it has been personally determined that a given revelation is authentic, the one who has received the revelation should accept it in the spirit of faith, and if the private revelation contains any message for others, those persons have an obligation to accept the truth of the revelation and act upon it.[5]

According to Miravalle, the fourth category is the highest level of evaluation and includes a "positive affirmation" by the church. Apparitions in this category would be officially approved or recognized by the church as "worthy of pious belief" (though still not a guarantee of the apparitions' authenticity). Approved apparitions have been judged as exhibiting characteristics that show forth the intervention of the divine.

Apparitions that reach categories three and four don't happen often. In fact, an article on apparitions in *U.S. News & World Report* stated: "During the past 160 years, the Catholic Church authenticated 14 apparitions as 'worthy of pious belief.'"[6] If an apparition falls under categories three or four it is considered to be church approved. This is sometimes true of those in category two (e.g., Guadalupe). The specific differences between category three (negative approbation) and category four do not seem to be clearly spelled out.

11

A Survey
of Marian Apparitions

aving some appreciation for how the Catholic church evaluates apparitions, we will examine six different claimed apparitions of Mary. The church's response to these six apparitions covers the four categories mentioned in the previous chapter. To examine each of these alleged supernatural appearances we will first review the historical events of the apparition—its claimed identity as well as any messages connected to it. Second, we will consider the influence the specific apparition has today (shrines, pilgrimages, etc.). Finally, we will note the church's response to each specific apparition.

Guadalupe, Mexico, 1531

Ten years after the conquest of Mexico by the Spaniards in 1521, Juan Diego, an Indian and recent convert to Catholicism, claimed to have seen and talked with the Virgin Mary. This religious experience would greatly influence Mexico and all of Latin America.

On December 9, 1531, while walking to church, Diego supposedly saw a brilliant vision of a young woman at Tepeyac, a hill northwest of present Mexico City. The radiating apparition spoke to Diego in Nahuatl, his own dialect, and identified herself as none other than the Virgin Mary, the blessed Mother of God. Diego, a man more than fifty years old, was ecstatic when he learned the identity of the radiant woman. She instructed him to have the bishop of Mexico construct a sanctuary at Tepeyac, which would be a sign of her motherly love and compassion for the people. Diego, convinced that he had conversed with the true mother of God, eagerly set out to see the bishop.

Upon finding Juan de Zumarraga, the newly appointed Bishop of New Spain, Diego communicated the apparition's message. The bishop was naturally skeptical and gave the story little credence. Three days later, during a second encounter with the apparition, Diego asked for a sign that would convince the bishop of his story's authenticity. The woman instructed him to fill his cloak *(tilma)* with roses, which were blooming unnaturally in December, and take them to the bishop. When the seer unrolled his cloak before the bishop, a permanent image of the Virgin Mary was imprinted on his cloak. The bishop accepted this as a genuine sign of the Virgin's presence to the people of Mexico. This tradition is the basis for popular devotion to the one known as Our Lady of Guadalupe.[1]

The first sanctuary at Guadalupe was erected around the year 1533. In 1709 a basilica was built that displayed Juan Diego's *tilma* with the famous image on it. In 1976 a new basilica was built and dedicated in Mexico City, with the old one still standing.

The story of the apparitions of Our Lady of Guadalupe has been extremely popular, particularly in Mexico and the rest of Latin America. In 1737 the Lady of Guadalupe was named Patroness of the City of Mexico, and in 1910 Pope Pius X declared her Patroness of all Latin America. In 1945, Pope Pius XII stated that the Lady of Guadalupe was the "Queen of Mexico and the Empress of the Americas."[2] While more than a dozen popes have expressed love and veneration for the image and its tradition, the apparitions have never been received officially as worthy of pious belief. Nonetheless, the high honors given the Lady of Guadalupe place it among those apparitions in the second category which receive "unofficial acceptance."

Millions of people come to Mexico to visit the basilica dedicated to Our Lady of Guadalupe. In fact, Pope John Paul II, in his first "apostolic journey," made a "pilgrimage of faith" to this shrine in January 1979. During his pilgrimage the pope addressed these words to the Mexican people: "I come to you bearing in my eyes and in my soul the Image of Our Lady of Guadalupe, your Protectrix. You bear a filial love toward her which I have been able to spot not only in her shrine but also while passing through the streets and cities of Mexico. Wherever there is a Mexican, there is the Mother of Guadalupe. Someone recently told me that 96 out of 100 Mexicans are Catholic but 100 out of 100 are Guadalupeans!"[3]

Lourdes, France, 1858

Possibly the most famous of the apparitions of Mary are associated with an obscure village known as Lourdes, in southwest France. Bernadette Soubirous, a fourteen-year-old illiterate girl from the poor village of Lourdes, claimed to have received eighteen apparitions of the Blessed Virgin Mary from February 11 to July 16, 1858.[4] These apparitions, which are known around the world, have had a profound influence on Marian devotion among Catholics.

The first apparition took place when Bernadette was standing near the rock formation known as the grotto of Massabielle. There she encountered a bright light which gradually revealed a lady in white who was holding a rosary. While the apparition did not

Apparitions of the Virgin Mary

speak, the lady smiled at Bernadette and motioned for her to come closer. This is how Bernadette recalled it:

> I saw a Lady in white, she was wearing a white dress and a blue sash and a yellow rose on each foot the color of the chain of her Rosary. . . . I put my hand in my pocket, I found my Rosary in it, I wanted to make the sign of the cross, I could not get my hand up to my forehead; it fell back, the vision made the sign of the cross, then my hand shook, I tried to make it and I could, I said my Rosary, the vision ran the beads of hers through her fingers but she did not move her lips, when I finished my Rosary, the vision disappeared all of a sudden.[5]

Over a five-month period Bernadette received numerous messages from this lady that had two primary emphases. First was the need for prayer, especially the reciting of the rosary. Emphasis on the rosary was evidenced by the fact that the apparition herself appeared with a rosary in hand. The second emphasis was the urgent need of offering penance to God for the conversion of sinners. This call was revealed through the apparition's request that Bernadette perform such penitential acts as walking on her knees, eating grass, and drinking from a spring that Bernadette discovered through direction from the apparition.[6]

Along with the messages, the apparition disclosed three so-called secrets to Bernadette, which she was forbidden to reveal. The apparition also stated that the priests should allow the people to come in procession to the site of the apparition and that a chapel should later be built there.

During earlier apparitions to Bernadette, the lady had been reluctant specifically to reveal her identity. However, during the sixteenth apparition, which took place on March 25, 1858, the feast day of the annunciation, she finally responded to Bernadette's persistent pleas, described by Bernadette:

After having poured out my heart to her I took up my Rosary. While I was praying, the thought of asking her name came before my mind with such persistence that I could think of nothing else. I feared to be presumptuous in repeating a question she had always refused to answer. And yet something compelled me to speak. At last, under an irresistible impulse, the words fell from my mouth, and I begged the Lady to tell me who she was. The Lady did as she had always done before; she bowed her head and smiled but she did not reply. I cannot say why, but I felt myself bolder and asked her again to graciously tell me her name; however she only bowed and smiled as before, still remaining silent. Then once more, for a third time, clasping my hands and confessing myself unworthy of the favour I was asking of her, I again made my request. . . . At the third request her face became very serious and she seemed to bow down in an attitude of humility. Then she joined her hands and raised them to her breast. . . . She looked up to heaven. . . . then slowly opened her hands and leaning forward towards me, she said to me in a voice vibrating with emotion: "I am the Immaculate Conception!"[7]

The Lady of Lourdes had identified herself by referring to the Catholic dogma that had been defined by the church only four years before. On December 8, 1854, Pope Pius IX declared the immaculate conception to be an official dogma of the church. From his bull *Ineffabilis Deus* we read: "We declare, pronounce and define that the most blessed Virgin Mary, at the first instant of her conception was preserved immaculate from all stain of original sin." Obviously, by giving such a response the Lady of Lourdes claimed to be the Blessed Virgin Mary, the mother of Jesus Christ.

The apparitions were confirmed by the church in 1862 (only four years after they occurred—an unusually brief period of evaluation) and the public cult of Our Lady of Lourdes was sanctioned.[8] The apparitions at Lourdes actually received the church's negative approval.[9] This is the third category, mentioned above, in which the church states that there is "nothing contrary to

Catholic faith or morals." Some of the reasons cited in favor of the apparitions included medical cures associated with the apparitions, good spiritual effects resulting from the devotion, and the accuracy and reliability of Bernadette's testimony. Bernadette, who became a nun in 1865, died in 1879 and was canonized as a saint in 1933.[10]

Today, Lourdes remains one of the most popular Marian shrines in the world. This year alone more than five million people will visit the shrine, which will enrich the town nearly $400 million. Without a doubt its greatest appeal is the many physical healings claimed by people who have visited the shrine. The Medical Bureau of Lourdes, which investigates reported healings, has stated that by 1988 more than sixty miraculous cures were sanctioned by the church.[11] People who come to Lourdes frequently bathe in the grotto spring, which is reputed to bring about healing. So many people are coming to Lourdes, in fact, there is now a shortage of water; Lourdes has actually had to ration its holy water.[12]

Fatima, Portugal, 1917

Millions of people make pilgrimages to the mountainous town of Fatima every year. The shrine at Fatima, located in central Portugal, rivals Lourdes as one of the most famous Marian shrines in the world. It commemorates the Virgin's reported appearances to three children on six different occasions from May 13 to October 13, 1917.[13]

The three poor shepherd children, Lucia dos Santos, ten years old, and her cousins Jacinta and Francisco de Jesus Marto, ages seven and nine, said that they saw the brilliant figure of a lady standing on a cloud above some trees. The lady requested that the children return to that place on the thirteenth of each month until October, when she would reveal her identity and make known her requests. Lucia gives an account of the first apparition:

High up on the slope in the Cova da Iria, I was playing with Jacinta and Francisco. . . . We had only gone a few steps further when, there before us on a small holmoak [tree], we beheld a lady all dressed in white. She was more brilliant than the sun, and radiated a light more clear and intense than a crystal glass filled with sparkling water, when the rays of the burning sun shine through it.

We stopped, astounded, before the apparition. We were so close, just a few feet away from her, that we were bathed in the light which surrounded her, or rather, which radiated from her. Then Our Lady spoke to us:

Lady: "Do not be afraid. I do you no harm."

Lucia: "Where are you from?"

Lady: "I am from heaven."

Lucia: "What do you want of me?"

Lady: "I have come to ask you to come here for six months in succession, on the 13th day, at this same hour. Later on, I will tell you who I am and what I want."

After a few moments, Our Lady spoke again: "Pray the Rosary every day, in order to obtain peace for the world, and the end of the war."

Then she began to rise serenely, going up towards the east, until she disappeared in the immensity of space.[14]

One of the central messages of the apparitions at Fatima is the call to world peace. The reference to the "end of the war" in the first apparition refers to the First World War, which in 1917 was still raging in Europe. During one of the apparitions, a prediction was made that the First World War would come to an end, but that another one would soon break out. Additionally, a prediction was made regarding Russia, that it would "spread its errors throughout the world, causing wars and persecutions of the church." The only way to avert such a bleak future, according to the message of Fatima, was to have people pray and do penance to God for the worldwide conversion of sinners. It should be noted, incidentally,

Apparitions of the Virgin Mary

that many Catholics give credit to the Virgin for the ultimate fall of Soviet Communism.

The messages of prayer, penance, and conversion were similar to the messages given at Lourdes. However, the message of Fatima in the second apparition specified just how the world was to be converted: through daily recitation of the rosary and by worldwide devotion to the "Immaculate Heart of Mary." While the rosary is discussed in detail in chapter 14, Marian scholar Mark Miravalle explains briefly the significance of devotion to Mary's immaculate heart in the Fatima apparitions:

> The message of the second apparition offers a considerable contribution to the development of the fundamental Marian call to prayer and penance for reparation and conversion. Here Mary states that it is the wish of Christ that his Mother is more greatly known and more greatly loved throughout the world, to be specifically promulgated through a world devotion to his Mother's Immaculate Heart, symbol both of her maternal love for all humanity and for the pains suffered by that maternal Heart from the outrages committed against her by the very objects of her love, her earthly children. The message goes on to present her Immaculate Heart as a spiritual refuge in the midst of a temporal suffering and hardship. Mary accentuates the role of her Immaculate Heart as having essentially a role of intercession, as a Christ-intended path bringing the wayfarer to salvation, and never as a devotion that poses the Immaculate Heart as its own final goal.[15]

The second apparition calls on people to consecrate themselves to Mary's immaculate heart, that is, to give themselves totally to God through Mary's immaculate heart. The Gospels, we are told, contain references to Mary's pure and loving heart: "But his mother treasured all these things in her heart" (Luke 2:19, 51). Since Mary put herself totally at God's disposal and was obedient to God's requests, Catholics argue that she can also help others to give themselves solely to God. Consecration to Mary's heart is to allow Mary to use her full powers of intercession in and through a person's life to draw him or her to God. Mary is seen as a mother who is uniting her children.

Just as in the apparitions at Lourdes, the Lady of Fatima gave the children secrets concerning the future. The messages of Fatima are interpreted as being apocalyptically urgent. Will people respond to her call for prayer (primarily the rosary), penance, conversion, and peace?

Each monthly apparition revealed more of the lady's desires. During the third apparition she showed the children visions of hell; in the fourth she requested that a chapel be built on the site of the appearances; but it is the sixth apparition for which Fatima is most famous.

During the sixth apparition the lady revealed her identity: "I am the Lady of the Rosary." Following the apparition celestial miracles reportedly took place in the presence of thousands. The *New Catholic Encyclopedia* describes the sixth apparition and the miraculous events which followed it: "On that date, in wet and dismal weather, she announced to them that she was Our Lady of the Rosary, and called for amendment in men's lives. Then the sun appeared and seemed to rumble, rotate violently, and finally fall, dancing over the heads of the throng before it returned to normal. Many of the crowd reported having seen this 'Miracle of the Sun' that was repeated twice more."[16]

In 1930, the apparitions at Fatima received the church's negative approbation, the same evaluation given to Lourdes. Fatima has received the official praises of Popes Pius XII and Paul VI. As well, numerous magazines are dedicated to Fatima's Our Lady of the Rosary.

Fatima's greatest advocate, however, would seem to be the present pope, John Paul II. Not only has the pope visited Fatima several times, he has also publicly given credit to "Our Lady of Fatima" for saving his life during a failed assassination attempt which took place in St. Peter's Square on May 13, 1981.[17]

Just before the pope was shot by would-be assassin Mehmet Ali Agca, he had bent over to acknowledge a little girl who was wearing a small picture of "Our Lady of Fatima" around her neck. It is reported that the pope now believes that if he had not bent over to recognize the girl, the assassin's bullets would have struck him in the head and killed him. Coupling this with the fact that the assassination took place on the anniversary of the beginning of the Fatima apparitions (May 13), the pope has come to believe that his life and mission as pope are directly connected to one of the revealed secrets of the Fatima apparitions.

While Marian apparitions are considered options which can be accepted or rejected by individual Catholics, it is significant to note that the undisputed head of Catholicism has a strong commitment to Marian apparitions (at least to Guadalupe, Lourdes, and Fatima) and has even accepted some of the messages as being revelatory. This provides a powerful contemporary example of how Marian apparitions continue to influence Roman Catholicism.

Beauraing and Banneux, Belgium, 1933

Two of the most recent ecclesiastically recognized apparitions of Mary took place in the small towns of Beauraing and Banneux in Belgium. In Beauraing, sixty miles southeast of Brussels, five children from two families claimed to have received thirty-three apparitions of the Virgin Mary covering the period from November 29, 1932, to January 3, 1933. The apparition identified herself as "the Immaculate Virgin," "the Mother of God," and "the Queen of Heaven."[18]

In Banneux, it was reported, Mariette Beco, an eleven-year-old girl from a poor family, received eight apparitions of the Virgin Mary from January 15 to March 2, 1933. The young Mariette claimed that she first saw the apparition of Mary standing in the family vegetable garden. Over a number of weeks a beautiful lady dressed in a flowing white gown and holding a rosary appeared to her during the evening and claimed to be "the Virgin of the Poor."

While these apparitions are not nearly as popular as Lourdes and Fatima, in 1949 both of them were recognized as worthy of belief. In fact, according to one Marian scholar, they were given the rare "positive affirmation" of the church.

Bayside, New York, 1970

One of the most popular and controversial claims of Marian apparitions, at least in the United States, comes from the visionary experiences of Veronica Lueken of Bayside, New York.[19] Lueken, a New York housewife, claims that on April 7, 1970, she began receiving regular visits from the Blessed Virgin Mary. The apparitions took place outside of St. Robert Bellarmine Catholic Church in Bayside, Queens, New York.

According to Lueken, the Virgin announced that she would appear on the evening of major feast days of the church, especially those dedicated in her honor. Revealing herself as "Our Lady of the Roses, Mary Help of Mothers," the apparition requested that a shrine and basilica be built in her honor at the site of the apparitions.

The messages given at Bayside are very critical of many current trends within Catholicism. Lueken has spoken against the Catholic charismatic movement, the use of most modern Bible translations, and even the practice of receiving the eucharistic host in one's hand rather than in the mouth at communion. The messages frequently denounce many of the changes brought about by the Second Vatican Council in the mid-1960s.

Other messages have denounced abortion, occultic practices, and freemasonry. A consistent theme in the Bayside messages is that the world faces an imminent apocalyptic judgment because of the moral disintegration in society.

The Bayside apparitions were investigated by the Roman Catholic Diocese of Brooklyn. The diocese reported that there was nothing miraculous or sacred about the apparitions or messages connected with Bayside. In fact, the commission stated that the apparitions were inauthentic (category one), primarily because some of the messages challenged the authority of the church.[20]

Even though the apparitions of Bayside have been denounced as inauthentic by the local bishop, thousands of people still attend vigils at the supposed site of the apparitions. Lueken's alleged visions have been widely publicized, and literature concerning "Our Lady of the Roses" shows no sign of dying out.

The apparitions I have discussed above are only meant to serve as a survey to this provocative topic. There are a host of other apparitions that could be described, such as Rue du Bac, Paris (1830), La Salette, France (1846), Pontmain, France (1871), and Knock, Ireland (1879). Apparitions of Mary are now springing up around the globe. In fact, in recent years apparitions have been reported in Argentina, Spain, Egypt, Japan, Yugoslavia, the United States, and Africa.

12

The Mystery of Medjugorje

As the decade of the 1980s began, few people outside of Yugoslavia had heard of Medjugorje (pronounced Med-ju-gory-ah), a small and remote farming community nestled among the hills in the province of Hercegovina in what was then southwestern Yugoslavia.[1] In the summer of 1981, however, events transpired that would transform this once-obscure community into an international pilgrimage center. Over a ten-year period some ten to fifteen million people from five continents have journeyed to Medjugorje.[2] This is even more significant considering Yugoslavia was a communist country.

What could attract so many people to this out-of-the-way place? It is the startling claim of six Croatian young people that for the past decade they have communicated almost daily with an apparition that identifies itself as the Blessed Virgin Mary.[3]

The Beginning of the Apparitions

On Wednesday, June 24, 1981, two girls, Ivanka Ivankovic (age fifteen) and Mirjana Dragicevic (age sixteen), had gone out to a hillside behind their homes to smoke cigarettes. While walking down the rocky slopes of Podbrdo (pod-bre-do) Hill in the late afternoon, Ivanka looked up and saw the luminous figure of a young woman in a gray robe hovering three feet above the ground. "Look, Mirjana," Ivanka said excitedly, "it's the Gospa" (the Croatian word for Madonna, or Virgin Mary). Mirjana, seeing that her friend was genuinely startled, replied: "Don't be an idiot. Why on earth would the Gospa appear to the likes of us?"[4] Both girls were gripped with fear and ran down the hill to the village.

About an hour later, the two girls reluctantly agreed to go back up the hill to help a friend round up a small flock of sheep that had been grazing on Podbrdo. When they reached the same spot where Ivanka had first seen the apparition, all three girls saw a figure of a woman holding a child in her arms. Just then, a fourth teenage girl, Vicka Ivankovic (no relation to Ivanka), who had come looking for her friends, joined them. Vicka was especially terrified by the appearance of the woman and ran down the hill seeking help. Two teenage boys were summoned for support, and they witnessed the apparition as well. The radiant figure beckoned the youths to come toward her, but all six were shaken by the experience and ran down the hill to their homes. In Vicka's own words: "But then, all of a sudden, I looked up and saw her standing there, just as clearly as I can see you now. She wore a grey dress with a white veil, a crown of stars [around her head], blue eyes, dark hair and rosy cheeks. And she was floating about this high in the air on a grey cloud, not touching the ground. . . . She called us to go nearer, but none of us dared to."[5]

The youths told their families and friends about the apparition, but no one believed them. Some of the parents instructed their children to keep quiet concerning the incident, lest they be thought mad by their neighbors. Teasing, Vicka's sister suggested that they may have seen a flying saucer.

The next day, four girls and two boys encountered the apparition again at the same place on the hill. This group was slightly different from those who had seen the apparition the previous day. It included from the first day Ivanka, Mirjana, Vicka, and Ivan Dragicevic (age sixteen). The young people who joined the group on the second day were Marija Pavlovic (age sixteen) and a young boy, Jacov Colo (age ten). These six Croatian youths would become Medjugorje's permanent group of "visionaries" or "seers." They are the only people who can see the apparitions.

On this second day of the apparitions, it was again Ivanka who first saw the figure. As before, the luminous woman beckoned the children to come toward her. Still fearful, but nevertheless feeling strangely drawn to "the lady," the children rushed toward the glowing apparition, knelt down in front of it, and began to pray.

Still grieving from her mother's recent death, Ivanka was the first to speak: "Where is my mother?" The lady told the girl that her mother was well, that she was with her, and not to worry. Ivanka asked if her mother had left a message for her children. The lady responded: "Obey your grandmother and be good to her because she is old and cannot work."[6] Mirjana, being concerned with what others would say, complained openly: "Dear Gospa, they will not believe us when we go home. They will tell us that we are crazy." The lady merely smiled and promised to return the next day. "Go in the peace of God," was her benediction as she disappeared from sight. The apparition had lasted some ten to fifteen minutes.[7]

News about the apparitions spread like wildfire throughout Medjugorje and its surrounding areas. By Friday, the third day of the appearances, two or three thousand people joined the visionaries on the hill awaiting the apparition. A bright light reportedly flashed three times on the horizon just before the apparition appeared. The young people were much bolder now in approach-

Apparitions of the Virgin Mary

ing the mysterious lady. Vicka, the most outspoken of the visionaries, brought forth some holy water mixed with salt. She sprinkled the apparition, saying: "If you are really Our Lady, then stay with us. If not, leave us!" The lady only smiled in response. Then the following dialogue ensued:

Visionaries: Who are you?

Apparition: I am the Blessed Virgin Mary.

Visionaries: Why have you come here? What do you desire?

Apparition: I have come because there are many true believers here. I wish to be with you to convert and to reconcile the whole world.

Visionaries: Why are you appearing to us? We are not better than others.

Apparition: I do not necessarily choose the best.

Visionaries: Give us a sign which will prove your presence.

Apparition: Blessed are those who have not seen and who believe.

Visionaries: Will you come back?

Apparition: Yes, to the same place as yesterday.[8]

Following the dialogue, the lady joined with the young people in reciting several traditional Catholic prayers. Seven times they recited the "Our Father" (also known as the Lord's Prayer), the "Hail Mary" (with the lady not participating), and the "Glory Be to the Father." At the lady's insistence, they also recited the Apostle's Creed.[9] The lady's last words, as would be her custom, were "Go now in peace."

Shortly after the apparition ended, Marija, becoming separated from the others because of the crowd, received a personal apparition. In the midst of a radiant cross of light, the lady appeared weeping. "Peace, peace, only peace," the figure cried. "Reconcile yourselves. Peace must take place between God and man and between men."

The apparitions were drawing so much attention by the fourth and fifth days that the communist police immediately cracked down on the new movement. They dispersed the large crowds (15,000 persons were present on the hill during the fourth day of apparitions) and interrogated the visionaries. All six youths were submitted to rigorous medical and psychiatric examinations. But when the tests showed no sign of maladjustment, they were allowed to return to their homes. The police also ordered the priests of St. James Parish (the Catholic church in Medjugorje) to ban the apparitions. Ten days after the appearances had begun, Yugoslavian television condemned them as "a Croatian nationalist plot."[10] The communists suspected that the apparitions were really a front, intended to cover a politically motivated uprising.

The local Franciscan priests were initially very skeptical about the apparitions. Father Jozo Zovko, the newly appointed pastor of St. James Parish, at first thought the youths were using drugs. Zovko gradually grew to accept the visionaries' claims and sought to protect them from the police. In a private interview he informed me that he himself witnessed a silent apparition one night during mass. Shortly after his acceptance of the apparitions, Zovko was arrested for "inciting the crowds." He ended up serving eighteen months of a three-year prison sentence.

The police did their best to stop the phenomenon, but to no avail. As the visions continued, most of the villagers in and around Medjugorje began to be convinced of their authenticity. Because the communists did not allow religious services outside the church, the visionaries asked the lady if she would appear to them inside the church. Soon after their request they began receiving apparitions in the church rectory of St. James Parish. Except for a few apparitions in the visionaries' homes, the appearances have remained in the church.

What Do the Visionaries Claim to See?

The young people all attest that three flashes of light almost always precede the coming apparition. They also claim they see the Virgin Mary as a real, external person, occupying three-dimensional space. They describe her, just as Vicka did above, as a young woman wearing a gray robe and a white veil, having a crown of stars around her head, and having blue eyes, black curly hair, rosy cheeks, and floating on a cloud. The visionaries say the Virgin Mary speaks to them in their native language, Croatian, and that they can both hear and touch her. While they claim that they all see the same figure, sometimes the messages to particular visionaries are individual and private.

They also claim that other persons have appeared to them, including various angels, Jesus, the devil, and certain relatives who have died. They have further reported that they were given the opportunity to see visions of heaven, purgatory, and hell.[11]

Twenty-Five Hundred Apparitions and Counting

The tenth anniversary of the apparitions having passed, it is extraordinary that the visionaries still claim to witness apparitions nearly every day. While two of the original visionaries have stopped seeing daily visions (Mirjana and Ivanka), the other four, whose ages now range in the twenties, claim that the appearances continue. The total number of apparitions has reached approximately twenty-five hundred. This is in sharp contrast to the alleged apparitions at Lourdes, where St. Bernadette was said to have received only a total of eighteen apparitions over a period of five months. Similarly, at Fatima there were only a handful of reported apparitions over a period of several months.

One Thousand Messages

Over this eleven-year period the visionaries claim to have received roughly a thousand messages from the Blessed Virgin

Mary. According to Catholic scholar Mark Miravalle the overall messages of Medjugorje fall into these four basic divisions: personal dialogue, the secrets, information for later disclosure, and the principal messages.[12]

The messages described as *personal dialogue* are the personal discussions between the visionaries and the lady. This information is given privately to the visionaries and most likely concerns the affairs of their daily lives.

The *secrets* consist of ten messages the lady has promised to give to all the visionaries. This aspect of the messages is similar to the apparitions both at Lourdes and Fatima, where secrets were also given. The secrets are generally apocalyptic in nature and are said to affect the entire world. One of the secrets has already been partially disclosed by the visionaries: the lady has promised to leave a visible sign on the hill to commemorate the apparitions. The secrets consist of both blessings for the obedient and punishment for the wicked. The ninth and tenth secrets are spoken of as particularly grave for mankind. Mirjana and Ivanka claim to know all ten of these secrets. The other four visionaries know only nine. It is presumed that once all the visionaries have received the ten secrets, the apparitions will cease in Medjugorje, just as they have already ceased for Mirjana and Ivanka. In fact, the visionaries have all stated that, according to the lady, this will be her last appearance on the earth. This divulgence contributes to the messages' already apocalyptic orientation.

Information for later disclosure consists of information the visionaries have been instructed to disclose at the appropriate times in the future. It is commonly thought that the visionaries will reveal certain things to church authorities, possibly even to the Pope. Such disclosures will have some connection to the secrets and will serve as a way of verifying the predictive aspect of the secrets.

The fourth division, the *principal messages*, is considered the most important. These messages are universal in their scope and application. According to Miravalle, they contain six foundational themes: (1) faith (both in God and in the authenticity of the apparitions); (2) prayer (especially the rosary); (3) fasting (twice a week on bread and water); (4) penance (self-denial for the sake of lost souls); (5) conversion (to God and away from sin); and (6) peace (of the soul first, then of the world).

The call for peace appears to be the focal point in the Medjugorjian message, so much so that the lady reportedly identifies herself to the visionaries as the "Queen of Peace."[13]

Signs and Wonders

There have also allegedly been various signs and miracles that accompany the already supernatural apparitions in Medjugorje. The most popular is undoubtedly the "Miracle of the Sun" phenomenon. Rene Laurentin, an eminent Marian scholar, stated that "on numerous occasions, thousands have witnessed the sun change colors, spin, become a silver disc, throb and pulsate in the sky, and throw off a rainbow of colors."[14] When I visited Medjugorje in September 1990, I observed thousands of people looking directly into the sun every day at 5:45 P.M., when the apparition was allegedly taking place.

Most pilgrims claim that a part of the miracle is that they are able to observe the sun for several minutes without suffering any damage to their eyes. This is not true in everyone's case, however. The *New England Journal of Medicine* featured an article on people who have suffered serious eye damage from watching the sun while in Medjugorje.[15] Because it is happening rather frequently, some doctors have even begun calling it the "Medjugorje affliction."

In addition to the phenomena of the sun, unusual things have reportedly taken place in connection with a large cross at the top of Mount Krizevac, the highest peak in the area. This twenty-foot cement cross, which overlooks Medjugorje, was built in 1933 to commemorate the nineteen-hundredth year since Christ's death and resurrection. Some pilgrims have testified that they have seen the arms of the cross mysteriously spin. Others say that the cross frequently becomes a column of light more intense than a neon cross. Still others claim that they have seen the concrete cross disappear completely before their very eyes. It has also been reported that the word *mir* (the Croatian word for peace) has appeared in bright letters in the sky above the cross.

Other extraordinary events have been reported, including rosaries allegedly turning a gold or copper color, fires on the hillside with nothing being scorched, images of Jesus and Mary seen in the sky, and numerous claims to physical healings.[16]

Many Catholics who have visited this remote village, however, would say that the miraculous events are not the reason they are persuaded that Mary is appearing in Medjugorje. They are persuaded by the spiritual fruit they see present there. This fruit, in their thinking, is evidenced in the changed lives of those who visit Medjugorje and are challenged to live the simple but relevant messages given there.

The Catholic Church's Judgment

The happenings in Medjugorje are unique among reported apparitions, if only for their duration and frequency. After a decade of these apparitions, just what is the Vatican's attitude toward them? The answer to that question remains unclear. The Catholic church has not yet made an official pronouncement with regard to the claimed apparitions at Medjugorje. This does not mean, however, that the church has not been actively investigating the matter. Far from it.

According to church canon law, the responsibility for investigating an alleged apparition rests with the local bishop. In this case, he is Bishop Pavao Zanic of Mostar-Duvno, the prelate (high-ranking clergyman) of the diocese in which Medjugorje lies. Shortly after the apparitions began in Medjugorje, Zanic began looking

Apparitions of the Virgin Mary

into the events. Though always cautious, his initial findings confirmed the need for further study.

In 1982, Zanic headed an official diocesan commission to investigate the phenomenon. A fifteen-member panel studied it for five years before reaching a conclusion. Their findings were reportedly negative (against Medjugorje), but the results were never made public. The majority of the panel, made up of nearly a dozen theologians and two psychiatrists, voted against a supernatural explanation of the events. Bishop Zanic informed me during a private interview that the results of the voting were as follows: two votes that the supernatural was confirmed; one vote that there was something supernatural, but only in the beginning; one abstention; and eleven votes that the supernatural was not confirmed.

Bishop Zanic told me that he found serious discrepancies among the visionaries' testimonies. He affirmed that he caught them in clear fabrications, and that the alleged healings and miracles were either fraudulent or grossly exaggerated. He also stated that the local Franciscans had been guilty of disobedience and, in some cases, unethical practice. His conclusion is that the apparitions in Medjugorje are a fraud perpetuated by the local Franciscans, with whom he has been feuding. According to Zanic, the apparitions must be denounced as invalid, or they will ultimately bring scandal and disgrace upon the church. In a recent pamphlet the Bishop writes:

> What have they done to you Our Lady! For nine years they have been dragging you along as a tourist attraction. They have been speaking with you whenever it pleased them, as if you were a bank teller. They have fabricated messages, and they say that you come and appear there, but beyond their own arguments they have nothing to prove that what they say is true. The whole world is in expectation of a "great sign" and the naive still wait and believe. Unfortunately this false sensation will bring great disgrace and scandal upon the Church.[17]

In April 1986, Zanic brought his report to Joseph Cardinal Ratzinger, the prefect (official) of the Congregation for the Doctrine of the Faith in Rome (the ultimate deciding body with regard to apparitions). Cardinal Ratzinger decided that the conditions surrounding the apparitions at Medjugorje warranted a broader examination. In some ways, just the popularity of Medjugorje itself has demanded a more extensive evaluation. In addition, the long-standing conflict between Bishop Zanic and the Franciscans is well known. Some have voiced the possibility that this dispute (i.e., concerns that it may have biased the investigation) influenced Ratzinger's decision to have Bishop Zanic's diocesan commission dissolved. Ratzinger then transferred the authority for rendering a judgment on Medjugorje to the Bishops' Conference of Yugoslavia, presided over by Cardinal Kuharic, Archbishop of Zagreb, Yugoslavia. The bishops' conference installed a new commission, which has been investigating Medjugorje for the past several years. Their evaluation has progressed slowly, but in late November 1990, they released this controversial statement:

> From the very beginning, the bishops have been following the events of Medjugorje through the local bishop, the bishop's commission and the commission of the bishops' conference of Yugoslavia for Medjugorje. On the basis of studies that have been made to this moment, it cannot be affirmed that supernatural apparitions and revelations are occurring here.[18]

The meaning of this statement is open to interpretation. Opponents of Medjugorje argue that if nothing supernatural has been confirmed after ten years of investigation, then the apparitions are not genuine. They tend to see this statement as leading to a final negative verdict on Medjugorje. Supporters of the apparitions, however, believe that this statement is not the final word on Medjugorje; the validity of the apparitions is still an open question. Miravalle, for example, argues that the statement merely commu-

Apparitions of the Virgin Mary

nicates that nothing supernatural has been confirmed *as yet,* leaving the door open on the matter. It appears that both sides are still awaiting an official word from the Vatican. Recently, however, Cardinal Ratzinger has issued a reminder to the pilgrims that Medjugorje has not yet been approved by the church, and that it is forbidden for pilgrimages to be sponsored by the church: no one has the authority to sponsor a pilgrimage to Medjugorje in the name and through the funding of the church.[19]

Medjugorje's Leading Proponents

While the Catholic church has not yet made an unequivocal statement on the alleged apparitions, the same cannot be said for certain individuals. The topic of Medjugorje has become very controversial among Catholics. The apparitions have plenty of defenders and detractors.

Rene Laurentin

If Bishop Zanic is Medjugorje's strongest opponent, then world-renowned French Mariologist Rene Laurentin is its staunchest advocate. At present Laurentin has written some ten books on Medjugorje, including an exhaustive chronological survey of the messages. It was Laurentin's positive assessment as set forth in his book *Is the Virgin Mary Appearing at Medjugorje?* that gave scholarly credence to the apparitions.[20]

What does Laurentin think of Bishop Zanic's criticisms? Laurentin argues that Zanic's method of inquiry into the apparitions has been seriously flawed and that his criticisms are insignificant and slanted. He argues that Bishop Zanic's personal difficulties with the Franciscans have predisposed him against Medjugorje. Laurentin believes that the apparitions at Medjugorje pass all appropriate criteria for being considered authentic. In response to the Yugoslavian commission's statement, he said he still considers it an open question: "It can't be verified, but it is not excluded."[21]

Yet Laurentin says that he will submit to the church's final word on the matter.

Frane Franic

Another outspoken advocate of Medjugorje is retired Yugoslavian Archbishop Frane Franic. Archbishop Franic, an advocate of the charismatic renewal in Yugoslavia, has openly criticized Bishop Zanic's conclusions. In fact, the Vatican had to warn Zanic and Franic to stop publicly criticizing each other.

Franic believes that the spiritual fruit of Medjugorje, as seen in the changed lives of the villagers and pilgrims, is quite convincing. It is uncertain, however, whether any other Yugoslavian bishop shares Franic's conclusions.

It should also be noted that the apparitions are strongly supported by many within the Franciscan order. In America, several scholars from the Franciscan University at Steubenville—Mark Miravalle, John Bertolucci, Michael Scanlan—have publicly vocalized their support. Nevertheless, all of these scholars have stated that they will submit to the final judgment of the church.

Wayne Weible

Unique among Medjugorje's advocates is Wayne Weible. Weible, a journalist by trade, may be responsible for introducing more people in America to Medjugorje than any other person. The series of newspaper articles he wrote on Medjugorje in the 1980s contributed greatly to Medjugorje's growing popularity among Americans. Amazingly, more than fifteen million copies of these articles have now been distributed. Weible's book *Medjugorje: The Message* has become an overwhelming bestseller.

What makes Weible unique, however, is that he claims to be a Protestant. As a professing Lutheran, he does not think that the apparitions taking place in Medjugorje pose any threat to a biblically based faith. In fact, he believes these events are perfectly consistent with the teaching of the Bible.

I engaged Weible in an informal debate concerning Medjugorje on a Southern California radio program in 1991. On the program I asked Weible if, as a professing Protestant, he believed in the Protestant principle of *Sola Scriptura* (Scripture as the supreme authority). He denied it. In fact, Weible denied virtually all of the distinctive Protestant doctrines, including justification by grace through faith alone. The truth of the matter is that Weible is not a Protestant in his theology; rather he is a crypto-Catholic. Weible, in this author's opinion, actually misleads people when he states that he is a Protestant who endorses Medjugorje.

Why does Weible believe in the apparitions? He justifies his endorsement of Medjugorje on the basis of a personal mystical experience, not on a rational, critical investigation of the facts, or, for that matter, a careful analysis of Scripture. From a truly Protestant position, Weible's subjective approach to Medjugorje is simply unacceptable.

Slavko Barbaric

Of all the people who are closely connected to the apparitions, Father Slavko Barbaric is probably the most qualified to pass judgment on the occurrences. Barbaric, a Franciscan, is a trained theologian and psychotherapist and presently serves as spiritual advisor to the visionaries at St. James Parish. Amid a sea of tenderminded pilgrims, I found Father Barbaric very reflective and analytical in his approach to the apparitions.

I asked Barbaric in a private interview what led him to believe that these events are supernatural in origin rather than natural or psychological. He stated that what convinced him was the children's ordinariness. He did not think that the youths had been sophisticated enough to invent these things. I also asked him if the visionaries were emotionally and psychologically stable. It was Barbaric's professional opinion that they were psychologically sound and, in his own words, "simply normal young adults." This is in direct contrast to Bishop Zanic's claim that the visionaries are mentally ill.

Because of Barbaric's interaction with the visionaries over a period of several years, he believes that he can discount any explanation due to personal deceit, drugs, or psychosis. I also asked Father Barbaric if he had considered an occultic explanation—specifically, a manifestation of the demonic. He had, but he concluded that the good fruit of Medjugorje could only come from a good source (God). Jokingly he stated that if the devil was behind Medjugorje, then the devil has converted. To his knowledge, none of the youths had ever been associated with the occult.

Barbaric allowed me to interview the four persons who are still seeing the visions and to be present during an evening apparition at St. James Parish.

A Room with a View

On my last night in Medjugorje I was present during what is known as the "regular evening apparition." Father Barbaric allowed me to accompany him and Marija Pavlovic into an upstairs room in St. James Parish. I sat beside Marija when she experienced a vision. She began by kneeling on the floor and focusing her eyes on a crucifix hanging on the wall. She proceeded to recite the Lord's Prayer and then the Hail Mary in her native language of Croatian. After a few minutes her voice became inaudible (though she continued to speak), and she looked as if she were conversing with someone. For the next few minutes she would speak (inaudibly), and then at other times she appeared as if she were listening. Her eyes blinked on several occasions as she appeared transfixed for about four or five minutes. Her expression was very serious, although punctuated with a brief smile. Then she made the sign of the cross and began praying audibly again. Father Barbaric joined her in reciting several prayers before the experience ended.

The mood in the room throughout the experience was calm. Marija merely looked as if she were praying silently. I observed her carefully while at the same time I was praying for discernment. I saw nothing, and I sensed no other presence in the room except the three of us. Marija struck me as a quiet and devout Catholic woman. The experience was certainly one of the most interesting of my life.

Rivaling Lourdes and Fatima

As was stated earlier, since the apparitions began in 1981 Medjugorje has drawn ten to fifteen million people from five continents—in spite of the lack of church approval. Medjugorje has a truly international appeal. When I visited the village, I encountered large groups of Italians, French, Germans, Irish, Americans, and various Eastern Europeans. I also observed that the mass at St. James Parish was being said in six different languages. It is reported that more and more pilgrims from third world nations are also coming each year. Catholic journalist Gabriel Meyer stated that Medjugorje "is unquestionably the late 20th century's most remarkable Marian movement."[22]

This is supported by the media coverage it has received. Nearly all of America's news magazines—*Newsweek, Time, Life, U.S. News & World Report*, and *Insight*—and newspapers have reported on the alleged visitations of Mary, not to mention the international press. Television has also covered the events in Medjugorje: ABC's news program *20/20* carried a segment on the apparitions, and the BBC aired the popular film *The Madonna of Medjugorje*.

Among American Catholics, Medjugorje is "hot." Across the nation are nearly one hundred "Medjugorje centers" which distribute a myriad of books, tapes, newsletters, articles, and religious objects about the apparitions. Conferences on Medjugorje are very popular, drawing thousands. Charismatic Catholics especially appear to be attracted. Indeed, Gabriel Meyer estimates that 40 percent of the Catholics who visit Medjugorje are charismatic.

Unofficial pilgrimages to Medjugorje by American Catholics have been very popular since 1986. However, Yugoslavia's recent political strife, which has led to an all-out civil war, has significantly reduced the flow of American pilgrims since the summer of 1991. Nevertheless, interest in Medjugorje among American Catholics shows no sign of dying out. In fact, as of February 1992, the *Bookstore Journal's* list of best-selling Catholic books was topped by five books on Medjugorje.

Medjugorje attracts more than just Catholics, however. The former Yugoslavia's population was made up of a large number of Eastern Orthodox and Muslims as well as Roman Catholics. Many Orthodox and even some Muslims have visited Medjugorje.

Many observers (including myself) feel that Medjugorje's popularity will have some influence on the Vatican's final decision as to whether the apparitions should be approved. (The region's current political problems may significantly delay that decision, however.) Regardless of the church's final pronouncement, numerous Catholics already view Medjugorje as the continuation of Lourdes and Fatima. Medjugorje has had a real and substantial impact on millions of Catholics throughout the world.

Outspoken Medjugorje visionary Vicka Ivankovic with Kenneth R. Samples.

Visionary Ivan Dragicevic addresses hundreds of pilgrims in Medjugorje.

Kenneth R. Samples in front of St. James Parish. Apparitions of Mary have reportedly taken place within the church almost daily since 1981.

Statue of Mary in St. James Parish commemorating "Our Lady, Queen of Peace."

Father Slavko Barbaric, advocate of the Medjugorje apparitions. A trained theologian and psychotherapist, Father Barbaric serves as the visionaries' spiritual advisor.

A stained glass window in St. James Parish depicting the Virgin Mary appearing to the six children of Medjugorje. Even the church's architecture has been influenced by the apparitions.

Kenneth R. Samples with Bishop Pavao Zanic, the strongest opponent of the Medjugorje manifestations.

13

How Apparitions Have Influenced Catholic Piety

Having surveyed several diverse examples of Marian apparitions we shall consider how Marian apparitions have influenced Catholic devotional life.

The Rosary

The reciting of the so-called Dominican rosary is one of the most popular and recognizable forms of prayer in the Catholic church. The rosary is considered a pious practice that is intended to combine both vocal and contemplative prayer. Praying the rosary consists of reciting fifteen decades (or sets of ten) of "Hail Marys," each preceded by an "Our Father," and followed by a "Glory be to the Father." The vocal prayers are accompanied by meditations on certain aspects of the life of Jesus and Mary, referred to as "mysteries." The worshiper recites the vocal prayers, but dwells on the mysteries assigned to the decade he or she is reciting. The mysteries are separated into three divisions—joyful, sorrowful, glorious—with five meditations to each division. "Its fifteen mysteries, focusing attention on the Incarnation, sufferings, and glorification of Christ are a compendium of the life of Jesus and Mary and a summary of the liturgical year. Like the liturgy, the Rosary presents Christian truth comprehensively and graphically, and possesses great power to sanctify those who pray it. A prayer to Jesus and his Mother, it leads through Mary to Jesus, the source of all grace."[1]

The worshiper keeps track of these many prayers by the use of a string of beads, also called a rosary, to which a crucifix is attached. The central prayer of the rosary is certainly the "Hail Mary," which is repeated 150 times when the complete fifteen decades is recited. (Ordinarily, to "pray the rosary" means to pray only five of the fifteen decades.) The "Hail Mary" is recited in two parts, as follows:

> Hail Mary, full of grace, the Lord is with thee. Blessed art thou among women, and blessed is the fruit of thy womb, Jesus.

> Holy Mary, mother of God, pray for us sinners, now and at the hour of our death. Amen.

The origin of the rosary, at least St. Dominic's connection to it, has been vigorously debated. "Pious tradition" teaches that the Virgin Mary appeared to Dominic (d. 1221) in an apparition and gave him the rosary. She instructed him to proclaim its many benefits, and promised him many personal blessings if he did. This tradition has been around at least since the fifteenth century. It gained wide acceptance because of its insertion into many papal bulls and encyclicals, which promised various indulgences for those who faithfully recited the rosary.[2]

Linking the origin of the rosary to an apparition seen by St. Dominic has been disputed by modern Catholic scholars. The *New Catholic Encyclopedia* states that "those who have favored the tradition have not succeeded in mustering convincing proofs to support it."[3] Modern scholars further argue that the papal bulls and encyclicals that seemingly support the tradition were merely trying to foster devotion to the rosary, not to teach historical truth. It is generally accepted that while certain aspects of the modern rosary were in existence during St. Dominic's lifetime, the popular tradition has little or no historical support. The encyclopedia concludes by saying that "the most satisfying explanation of the Rosary's origin is that it developed gradually as various Christological and Marian devotions coalesced."[4] Nevertheless, many Catholics still believe this pious tradition.

While the origin of the rosary cannot be convincingly connected to an apparition of Mary, the command to pray the rosary is a central motif in nearly all of the ecclesiastically approved Marian apparitions. We saw in chapter 12 that this is especially true of the messages given at Lourdes and Fatima, where praying the rosary is one way of averting apocalyptic disaster. The Medjugorjian message follows this same pattern. During one of the apparitions at Medjugorje, the lady requested that the full fifteen-decade rosary be said every day. On June 25, 1985, the fourth anniversary of the apparitions, the following message was given: "Dear children, I ask you to ask everyone to pray the rosary. With the rosary you will overcome all the troubles which Satan is trying to inflict on the Catholic Church."[5] Six weeks later a similar message was given: "Dear children, today I call you to pray against Satan in a special way. Satan wants to work more now that you know he is active. Dear children, put on your armor against Satan; with rosaries in your hands you will conquer."[6] According to Mark Miravalle, the rosary is the fundamental form of devotional prayer requested in the Medjugorjian message.

Apparitions have even contributed new words to the rosary. Following the apparitions at Fatima in 1917, the prayer allegedly taught by the Virgin to the Fatima children is frequently added when reciting each decade: "O my Jesus, forgive us our sins, save us from the fires of hell, lead all souls to heaven, especially those in greatest need."[7]

Apparitions of Mary have thus done much to increase the popularity of the rosary among Catholics. Most Protestants, on the other hand, believe that the rosary, especially the "Hail Mary," is an inappropriate and unbiblical form of prayer. While the first stanza of the "Hail Mary" comes directly from Scripture (Luke 1:28), the context of the statement is the angel Gabriel giving a greeting to Mary. The "Hail Mary," however, turns this angelic greeting into a prayer—a prayer by human beings to another human being, albeit an exalted and glorified human. Protestants believe that the "Hail Mary" prayer is therefore used inappropriately—since prayer is only addressed to God in Scripture—and out of its biblical context (for more on this see chapter 8).

Protestants are further disturbed by the fact that the second stanza assumes that Mary is holy (sinless) and capable of making intercession on a person's behalf. Protestants have seen these assumptions as a challenge to Jesus Christ's unique holiness and mediatorship. While the rosary is a very popular prayer among Catholics, it is a stumbling block for most Protestants.

Scapulars

Another object of Catholic devotion that is attributed to a Marian apparition is the scapular. Scapulars are worn devoutly by millions of Roman Catholics throughout the world.

The first scapulars were worn by monks as early as the eleventh century to protect their habits (religious dress) while they performed manual labor. Initially they consisted of a large cloth worn over the shoulders (*scapular* is Latin for "shoulder"). Today, however, they are made up of two small double squares of cloth suspended from the shoulders by two strings or cords and worn under the clothing. Over a period of time symbolic meanings were attached to the garments: they were considered by some as a kind of cross worn around the shoulders, understood as a sign of God's protection. Others interpreted the scapular symbolically as a yoke in light of Jesus' command, "Take up my yoke and follow me." Now close to twenty different scapulars are connected to various religious orders.

The oldest and best known of the Marian scapulars is the brown scapular dedicated to Our Lady of Mount Carmel. Its origin is allegedly connected to a Marian apparition. The *New Catholic Encyclopedia* explains: "According to Carmelite legend, Our Lady appeared to St. Simon Stock in Cambridge in 1251 and, showing him a brown scapular, declared that whoever wore it until death would be preserved from hell and on the first Saturday after his death would be taken by her to heaven."[8]

Historically, it is questionable whether this apparition or the scapular associated with it was known to the Carmelite friars in the mid-thirteenth century.[9] Some believe it was a pious invention of a later time.

The promise of deliverance from hell, however, has been a source of controversy. While theologians insist that the scapular is not to be regarded as securing salvation in and of itself (the interior disposition of the soul—being in the state of grace without mortal sin—must be considered primary), many Catholics nonetheless view the scapular as having a magical efficacy. For many Catholics its alleged connection to an apparition makes it a guarantee from heaven.

Marian apparitions have had a significant influence on Catholic piety, with the rosary and scapulars being just two examples. Other areas of Catholic piety and life which have been touched by Marian apparitions include shrines, pilgrimages, societies, hymns, and art.

14

A Protestant Evangelical Response

Because of their seemingly miraculous character, Marian apparitions present a challenge to the Protestant evangelical faith that needs to be addressed. It is therefore my intention in this concluding chapter to evaluate these occurrences from the historic Protestant position. In so doing, I must assume, rather than defend, the Protestant belief in the supreme authority of Scripture. Over the centuries countless theologians and authors have adequately defended that belief.[1]

It seems evident from studying this distinctly Catholic phenomenon that the only way one could justify belief in Marian apparitions (especially Lourdes, Fatima, and Medjugorje) is to accept completely the Roman Catholic view of Mary. That is, if these apparitions are authentic and are performed under the auspices of almighty God, then we are dealing with the Mary of Roman Catholic theology. For these apparitions do nothing but confirm distinctly Catholic beliefs about Mary. However, this is the central reason why Protestant evangelicals cannot accept these apparitions as being from God. To accept these apparitions is to accept an unbiblical view of Mary. For the evangelical Protestant, the clear teaching of Scripture must supersede any private revelations, especially those that are directly incompatible with the Bible.

Just as the Catholic church uses an *objective* criterion for accepting or rejecting apparitions (conformity to Catholic teaching: Scripture and Tradition), the Protestant does so also. For the Protestant, the phenomenon must conform to Scripture (especially to those central truths rediscovered and emphasized in the Reformation). Protestants, then, are no more closed minded (*apriorism*) to supernatural manifestations than are Catholics; we merely use a different and, from our perspective, more appropriate criterion.

The Reformation principle of *Sola Scriptura* (Scripture alone), upon which Protestantism stands, asserts that Scripture is the supreme authority in matters of doctrine. However, the Catholic affirmation of Mary's immaculate conception, her perpetual virginity, her bodily assumption into heaven, and her work as an intercessor all lack biblical support.[2] Further, there is no biblical basis for granting Mary such exalted titles as Queen of Heaven, Mother of the Church, and Queen of all Saints.

It is not just that these Marian beliefs lack biblical support (nonbiblical); some of them, in fact, undermine clearly defined scriptural doctrines (unbiblical). For example, the dogma of the immaculate conception directly contradicts the crucial biblical teaching of the universality of sin (Ps. 51:5; Rom. 3:23). What is of most concern to Protestants, however, is the way in which Mariology challenges the uniqueness of Christ's person and also detracts from the complete sufficiency of his work.

If there is doubt about this, consider how Catholic Mariology parallels Christology: (1) Jesus was born without sin, Mary was conceived without original sin; (2) Jesus lived a sinless life, Mary also remained sinless; (3) following his resurrection Jesus ascended into heaven, Mary was assumed bodily into heaven; (4) Jesus is a mediator, Mary is a mediatrix; (5) Jesus is the Redeemer, Mary is coredemptrix; (6) Jesus is the new Adam, Mary is the new Eve; (7) Jesus is the King, Mary is the queen. Even Protestant scholars who are sympathetic to Catholicism believe that these parallels can only threaten Christ's preeminence and blur his exclusive role as Redeemer and mediator[3] (1 Tim. 2:5; Heb. 2:16–18; 4:14–15; 7:25; 9:12–14; 10:1–10).

Catholic Mariology being an extension of Christology raises another area of concern for Protestants. While Catholic scholars insist that Mary is merely an exalted creature, in actuality her pristine nature and elevated role in the church align her more closely with Christ than with mankind. The concern is that Mary, by virtue of her exalted status, has actually become a semidivine being. The great Yale scholar Jaroslav Pelikan expresses this concern:

> In both birth and death, therefore, she is different from other people; in both birth and death she resembles her divine Son. The dogma of the catholic church has always run the danger of glorifying Christ so much that it cut him off from the humanity he was to save. Now the dogma of the Roman Catholic Church is running a similar danger in its Mariology. More and more, the attributes ascribed to her seem closer to those of Christ than to those of common mortals. She was conceived in a special way, she performs miracles, she intercedes for us, she was assumed into heaven.[4]

Because Catholic Mariology and Marian apparitions are inextricably woven together (Mariology provides the basis for potentially authentic apparitions), we must jettison both. If we are forced to reject the Catholic view of Mary on scriptural grounds, we cannot then accept Marian apparitions that simply espouse the same doctrinal errors. We Protestants, therefore, have a scriptural right to discount Marian apparitions *a priori*, simply because they fail our criterion.

The truth or falsity of apparitions is measured then by whether the phenomenon as a whole conforms to Scripture, not on how dramatic or sensational the experience may be. For the Protestant, apparitions could never confirm the truth of Catholic Mariology, which is unbiblical by its very nature.

Finding an Explanation

Any honest effort to provide a satisfying explanation for the phenomenon known as Marian apparitions will prove to be a complex and difficult task. I freely admit that I may not be able to account for everything connected to these unusual occurrences. Nevertheless, logically the origin or cause of Marian apparitions must be either natural or supernatural. There could be numerous natural explanations. These range from outright human deception, to psychological projection or hallucination (though this seems doubtful in the best-known cases), or even possibly to some physical or natural scientific cause. The cause could even be found in a combination of these factors. However, because of the unbiblical nature of Marian apparitions, if the cause is supernatural in origin then we can only be dealing with the demonic, not with God. I realize that this line of reasoning will be offensive to many Catholics; nonetheless, I believe it is a necessary theological inference.

But could Satan (and/or demons) really be behind such seemingly benign and miraculous occurrences? There seems to be clear scriptural evidence that the answer is yes. First, we are told that the devil "masquerades as an angel of light" (2 Cor. 11:14–15). He is also capable of performing "counterfeit miracles, signs and wonders" (2 Thess. 2:9–10), and near the end of the ages he will inspire false Christs and false prophets who will "perform great signs and miracles to deceive even the elect—if that were possible" (Matt. 24:24). The Book of Revelation speaks several times of how the "beast" and the "false prophet"—both extensions of

Satan—will perform "great miraculous signs" at the end time (Rev. 13:13; 16:14; 19:20). In addition to counterfeit miracles, he is also capable of predicting the future (sometimes with astounding accuracy, but often not) and declaring a way of salvation (Acts 16:16). His goal is always to deceive, to cause people to abandon their faith, and, ultimately, to lead the world astray (1 Tim. 4:1; Rev. 12:9).

How does this apply in the case of Medjugorje and other popular Marian apparitions? Satan's purpose behind this phenomenon might be to divert Catholics in general, and evangelical Catholics in particular (e.g., many Catholic charismatics), from a faith centered in Christ and the biblical elements in Catholicism to an emphasis on the more unbiblical and even cultic aspects of Catholicism (Mariology in general, penance, purgatory, veneration of saints, etc.). All of these cultic aspects are directly connected to apparitions. As long as the emphasis remains on these unbiblical things, Satan can afford to disguise his deceptive scheme by mouthing Christian theology (telling Mary's followers to pray the creed, teaching there is only one God, etc.).

It is clear from Scripture that Satan has both the means and the motive to orchestrate the unusual events we have considered in this book.

Legend, Delusion, or Psychosis?

It should be recognized that a number of alleged Marian apparitions are based upon very sketchy evidence. As we have seen, the *New Catholic Encyclopedia* suggests that the apparitions of Mary to St. Dominic (associated with the rosary) and to St. Simon Stock in 1251 (associated with the scapular) are virtually legends. As well, this same encyclopedia points out that the documentary basis for the famous apparition at Guadalupe, Mexico (1531) is not without problems, though certainly much more credible than those associated with St. Dominic and St. Simon Stock.

The Catholic church also admits that most so-called apparitions remain unverified and can probably be explained by natural means. Some are intentionally fraudulent, while others are caused by illness. Modern psychiatry has proposed that religious visions are frequently the result of psychological projection, hysteria, and/or hallucinations. Although an antisupernatural bias no doubt influences some of these explanations, yet they do seem to fit and adequately describe much visionary phenomena (biblical visions being an obvious exception).

Problems with Medjugorje

Before discussing the evident problems with Medjugorje, it should be stated that there are a couple of things that stand out positively about these particular apparitions. First of all, the visionaries strike me as believable. They appear to be normal young adults, certainly not psychologically unbalanced. As well, in some cases there does seem to be evidence of "good fruit" manifest at Medjugorje (e.g., reports of lives being changed for the better, people believing the creed).

These positive features, however, do not establish the authenticity of the apparitions. The visionaries' believability adds credibility to a *supernatural* explanation for the events, but it does not assure us that this supernatural source is of God. It is possible for well-adjusted people to be *sincerely* deceived. And if the apparitions are demonic in origin, then their good fruit is nothing more than an enticing delusion.

There are several reasons for concluding that the apparitions are not of God. Significant problems accompany the phenomena of Medjugorje, let alone the underlying theology. First, there are some inconsistencies in the visionaries' testimonies. On June 30, 1981 (the first week of the apparitions), the visionaries reported that the Gospa would appear only three more times. This definite mistake establishes that the visionaries *are capable* of misrepresenting the heavenly figure they claim to speak for (unless we are to assume that Mary herself was mistaken). Additionally, when the apparitions began, it was stated that there were five secrets. This was later changed to ten.

Laurentin has attempted to explain these apparent contradictions by arguing that the particular visionary who first set these numerical limits (Mirjana) was giving her own impression about the duration of the apparitions and secrets, rather than revealing a specific message from the lady. However, if the visionaries have difficulty distinguishing between the revealed messages themselves and their private impressions or interpretations of the messages, then the validity of the messages is undermined. If Mirjana's impression was wrong about how long the apparitions would last, then it is quite possible she has been wrong about other points as well.

There is also the problem that some messages sound pluralistic: they imply the validity of the idea that all religions lead to salvation. In 1981, a priest asked the visionaries: "Are all the religions good?" Their answer was that the lady says, "All religions are good before God." On another occasion a message came forth stating that "you are not true Christians if you do not respect other religions" and that "division among the religions is caused by man, not God."

Laurentin attempts to defend these statements by maintaining that the lady is only requesting tolerance among differing religions.[5] However, he cannot be certain of this, and even Vatican officials are concerned with these pluralistic-sounding messages. If these messages are not genuinely pluralistic in content (which their actual wording would seem to imply), they are at least ambiguous. And such ambiguity of itself, on such an infinitely important matter as the way to salvation, would render their divine origin extremely questionable.

Another troubling aspect of Medjugorje is that some of the visionaries have seen, talked to, and even touched people who have died. In Ivanka's case, she embraced and kissed her dead mother on several occasions. During an interview, Ivanka described these encounters with her mother: "I've seen my mother three times since she died! . . . My favorite time was the last time she was with the Blessed Mother. My mother came over to me. She put her arms around me and kissed me. She said, 'Oh, Ivanka, I am so proud of you.'"[6]

This sounds very similar to the occultic practice of necromancy, a practice the Bible explicitly condemns (Deut. 18:10–12; Isa. 8:19; 1 Chron. 10:13–14). While some may argue that this is not technically necromancy, because the dead are not conjured, still the visionaries are receiving information from the dead, which is entirely foreign to Scripture and very much like the occultic practice. I would also argue that Mary herself is among the dead. If this contact with spirits is really happening, from a biblical point of view we must conclude they are communicating with a demonic counterfeit.

The Miracles at Lourdes and Fatima

Many Catholics are convinced that Lourdes and Fatima are genuine apparitions of Mary because of the signs and wonders allegedly performed at those locations. However, as we've already seen, the truth or falsity of apparitions is measured by whether the phenomenon as a whole conforms to Scripture, not by how sensational or seemingly wonderful the experience might be.

It should also be recalled that the signs and wonders allegedly performed at Lourdes and Fatima could have been done by Satan. In fact, when one analyzes many of the alleged miracles that accompany Marian apparitions, they seem to be of a kind different from those found in Scripture. This is true of biblical miracles as a whole, as well as the miracles in Jesus' public ministry. When did Jesus ever make the sun dance or crosses spin? All of his miracles were done in the context of ministry (service of human needs for the glory of God). Biblical miracles had a strong practical aspect. More-over, when Jesus performed a miracle, it was not perceived by only a few people but by all who were present, even those who were against Jesus. In contrast, many of the miracles associated with Marian apparitions seem dramatic and sensational—attention-get-ting if you will—the kind of miracles that Jesus consistently *refused* to perform (Matt. 12:38–39). This is a good reason to at least sus-pect the source of these miracles.

We would do well to heed the warnings of Scripture: "Test everything. Hold on to the good" (1 Thess. 5:21). "Dear friends, do not believe every spirit, but test the spirits to see whether they are from God" (1 John 4:1). I do not believe that the occurrences at Medjugorje, to cite a contemporary example, have been ade-quately tested for signs of the demonic. Spraying holy water mixed with salt is not sufficient. Furthermore, since Scripture instructs us to test the spirits (both teaching and allegedly supernatural man-ifestations), the fact that the lady at both Lourdes and Fatima refused initially to identify herself raises great suspicion as to her real identity.

Some argue that the physical healings at Lourdes demonstrate that the apparitions are definitely from God. However, on a prac-tical level, I am convinced that millions of people, including many of the pilgrims at Lourdes, actually worship the Virgin—perhaps ignorantly, and certainly against official church teaching. This is idolatry. Where there is idolatry, satanic activity is certain (1 Cor. 10:14–22), and satanic healing is possible, as can be observed in many shamanistic religions. I am not saying this must be the case. But if some healings at Lourdes are genuinely supernatural, for the Protestant this possibility becomes a strong probability given the unbiblical nature of the message and its possible connection to necromancy.[7]

Even some Catholics are concerned with the extremes within Catholic Marian devotion. However, the indictment of Jaroslav Pelikan is generally true: "The theologians and bishops of the church, who ought to watch and to warn the faithful of the excesses in such piety, are actually the ones who encourage the excesses."[8] They do this when they exalt Mary far beyond the place given her in Scripture.

Whether the cause is demonic or human, the effect of this phenomenon is to lead people away from the truth of God's Word. In fact, if we are to succeed in guarding against this type of spiritual aberration, Holy Scripture must be our standard. Protestants have long argued that it is Catholicism's failure to accept and appropriately apply the supreme normative authority of Scripture that has allowed the doctrinal excesses found in Catholic Mariology. This is especially tragic, because the popularity of these apparitions demonstrates that millions of Catholics are sincerely hungry for spiritual truth. However, the truth that sets men free is found only in the Christ of the apostolic writings. Therefore, it is precisely because of this evangelical Protestants' regard for Christ and Scripture, as well as for the true honor of Christ's mother, that I must protest against Marian apparitions and the cult of the Virgin Mary.

Notes

Introduction: The Cult of the Virgin Revives

1. "Pope Issues Encyclical on the Virgin Mary as Prelude to Marian Year," *Orange County Register* (from the *New York Times* wire service), 26 Mar. 1987, sec. A.

2. See, for example, Xavier Rynne, *Vatican Council II* (four volumes in one) (New York: Farrar, Straus and Giroux, 1968), 160, 444; Michael McAteer, "Is Mary Overemphasized?" *The Toronto Star*, 21 Feb. 1987, sec. M.

3. Ann Matter of the University of Pennsylvania, quoted in Charles W. Bell, "Renewing the Faith in Mary," *Los Angeles Daily News*, 23 May 1982, sec. F.

4. Charlotte Low, "The Madonna's Decline and Revival," *Insight*, 9 Mar. 1987, 61.

5. See, for example, the *Christianity Today* editorial, "What Separates Evangelicals and Catholics?" 23 Oct. 1981, 12–15.

6. Bell.

7. Richard N. Ostling, "Handmaid or Feminist?" *Time*, 30 Dec. 1991, 62.

8. Low, 61.

Chapter 1: Divine Maternity

1. John H. Leith, ed., *Creeds of the Churches*, rev. ed. (Richmond, Va.: John Knox Press, 1973), 36.

2. Eamon R. Carroll, "Mary in the Documents of the Magisterium," in *Mariology*, Vol. 1, ed. Juniper B. Carol (Milwaukee: Bruce Publishing Company, 1955), 8.

3. F. J. Sheed, *Theology for Beginners*, 3d ed. (Ann Arbor, Mich.: Servant Books, 1981), 127.

4. Ludwig Ott, *Fundamentals of Catholic Dogma*, 4th ed., ed. in English by James Canon Bastible, trans. from the German by Patrick Lynch (Rockford, Ill.: TAN Books and Publishers, 1974), 197.

5. Michael O'Carroll, *Theotokos: A Theological Encyclopedia of the Blessed Virgin Mary* (Wilmington, Del.: Michael Glazier, 1982), s.v. "Cana."

Chapter 2: Perpetual Virginity

1. J. N. D. Kelly notes that "not only the Antidicomarianites [those who denied Mary's perpetual virginity] attacked by Epiphanitus and the Arian Eunomius openly taught that the 'brethren of the Lord' were Mary's sons by Joseph, but Basil of Caesarea, while criticizing the latter, implied that such a view was widely held and, though not accepted by himself, was not incompatible with orthodoxy." *Early Christian Doctrines*, rev. ed. (New York: Harper and Row, 1978), 494–95.

2. Eamon R. Carroll, "Mary in the Documents of the Magisterium," in *Mariology*, Vol. 1, ed. Juniper B. Carol (Milwaukee: Bruce Publishing Company, 1955), 10.

3. Karl Keating, *Catholicism and Fundamentalism: The Attack on "Romanism" by "Bible Christians"* (San Francisco: Ignatius Press, 1988), 283.

4. *Ibid.*

5. John Calvin, *Commentary on a Harmony of the Evangelists, Matthew, Mark, and Luke*, Vol. 1, trans. William Pringle (Grand Rapids: Baker Book House, 1979), 41.

Chapter 3: The Immaculate Conception

1. Eamon R. Carroll, "Mary in the Documents of the Magisterium," in *Mariology*, Vol. 1, ed. Juniper B. Carol (Milwaukee: Bruce Publishing Company, 1955), 14–15.

2. After explaining how Origen "feels quite free to say of Mary that there were occasions when she wavered in her faith," Lucien Deiss acknowledges that "in all these positions he assumes, Origen has no intention of putting forward a personal opinion; he seems, rather, only to *reflect the ideas of his time*" (emphasis added). *Mary, Daughter of Sion* (Collegeville, Minn.: The Liturgical Press, 1972), 210.

3. See Ludwig Ott, *Fundamentals of Catholic Dogma*, 4th ed., ed. in English by James Canon Bastible, trans. from the German by Patrick Lynch (Rockford, Ill.: TAN Books and Publishers, 1974), 203.

4. *Colliers Encyclopedia*, 1972 edition, s.v. "Mary the Blessed Virgin."

5. Carroll, 17.

6. See Ott, 201.

7. *Dogmatic Canons and Decrees* (Rockford, Ill.: TAN Books and Publishers, 1977), 183–84.

8. Michael O'Carroll, *Theotokos: A Theological Encyclopedia of the Blessed Virgin Mary* (Wilmington, Del.: Michael Glazier, 1982), s.v. "Full of Grace."

9. *Ibid.*, s.v. "Immaculate Conception."

10. Karl Keating, *Catholicism and Fundamentalism: The Attack on "Romanism" by "Bible Christians"* (San Francisco: Ignatius Press, 1988), 268–69.

11. Ott, 201.

Chapter 4: The Assumption

1. Eamon R. Carroll, "Mary in the Documents of the Magisterium," in *Mariology*, Vol. 1, ed. Juniper B. Carol (Milwaukee: Bruce Publishing Company, 1955), 28.

2. *Ibid.*

3. Victor Buksbazen, *Miriam, the Virgin of Nazareth* (Philadelphia: Spearhead Press, 1963), 196.

4. Karl Rahner, *Mary Mother of the Lord* (Wheathampstead, Hertfordshire: Anthony Clarke Books, 1963), 16.

5. Alfred C. Rush, "Mary in the Apocrypha of the New Testament," in Carol, *Mariology*, Vol. 1, 170–71.

6. Relative to the absence of any mention in Scripture of the assumption, an interesting admission is unknowingly made by Karl Keating. Writing about those Protestants who mistakenly believe the assumption means Mary never died, Keating states: "The Bible says nothing about what happened to Mary, they note, and does it not seem there would be some mention of her never dying? After all, it would have been truly remark-able'. [sic] *There is a certain sense in their argument*, and if the doctrine of the Assumption were what they think it is, *the argument would carry some weight*" (emphases added) (*Catholicism and Fundamentalism: The Attack on "Romanism" by "Bible Christians"* [San Francisco: Ignatius Press, 1988], 272–73). The Protestant can rejoin to Keating: "But can't the same objection be raised to the assumption as it is properly understood by you?" Certainly a *resurrected* body being carried up into heaven is as "remark-able" as a nondying one going the same route. Therefore, the Protestant objection to the assumption's lack of scriptural support does "carry some weight."

7. Pope Pius XII, *The Dogma of the Assumption* (*Munificentissimus Deus*) (New York: Paulist Press, 1951), 22.

8. Quoted in Michael O'Carroll, *Theotokos: A Theological Encyclopedia of the Blessed Virgin Mary* (Wilmington, Del.: Michael Glazier, 1982), s.v. "Assumption of Our Lady, The."

9. See Elliot Miller, "The Christian and Authority (Part One)," *Forward*, Spring 1985, 8–15. The author also plans to write a book on this theme in the near future.

Chapter 5: Spiritual Motherhood

1. For a detailed discussion of this, see G. C. Berkouwer, *The Second Vatican Council and the New Catholicism*, trans. Lewis B. Smedes (Grand Rapids: William B. Eerdmans Publishing Company, 1965), 221–48.

2. Lucien Deiss, *Mary, Daughter of Sion* (Collegeville, Minn.: The Liturgical Press, 1972), 213.

3. *Ibid.*, 214.

4. Quoted in Eamon R. Carroll, "Mary in the Documents of the Magisterium," in *Mariology*, Vol. 1, ed. Juniper B. Carol (Milwaukee: Bruce Publishing Company, 1955), 41.

5. Pope Pius X, *Mary Mediatrix* (encyclical letter *Ad Diem Illum*), translated and annotated by Dominic J. Unger (Paterson, N.J.: St. Anthony Guild Press, 1948), 7–8.

6. Quoted in Carroll, 42.

7. Victor Buksbazen, *Miriam, the Virgin of Nazareth* (Philadelphia: Spearhead Press, 1963), 204.

8. Michael O'Carroll, *Theotokos: A Theological Encyclopedia of the Blessed Virgin Mary* (Wilmington, Del.: Michael Glazier, 1982), s.v. "Mother of Divine Grace (The Spiritual Motherhood)."

9. F. J. Sheed, *Theology for Beginners*, 3d ed. (Ann Arbor, Mich.: Servant Books, 1958), 131–32.

Chapter 6: Coredemptrix and Mediatrix

1. Ludwig Ott, *Fundamentals of Catholic Dogma*, 4th ed., ed. in English by James Canon Bastible, trans. from the German by Patrick Lynch (Rockford, Ill.: TAN Books and Publishers, 1960), 215.

2. Karl Keating, *Catholicism and Fundamentalism: The Attack on "Romanism" by "Bible Christians"* (San Francisco: Ignatius Press, 1988), 279.

3. Quoted in Victor Buksbazen, *Miriam, the Virgin of Nazareth* (Philadelphia: Spearhead Press, 1963), 204.

4. Eamon R. Carroll, "Mary in the Documents of the Magisterium," in *Mariology*, Vol. 1, ed. Juniper B. Carol (Milwaukee: Bruce Publishing Company, 1955), 36.

5. *Ibid.*, 36.

6. Pope Pius X, *Mary Mediatrix* (encyclical letter *Ad Diem Illum*), translated and annotated by Dominic J. Unger (Paterson, N.J.: St. Anthony Guild Press, 1948), 8.

7. Quoted in Carroll, 37.

8. *Ibid.*, 38.

9. Quoted in Pius X, 28, from D. J. Unger's notes.

10. Ott, 212.

11. G. C. Berkouwer, *The Second Vatican Council and the New Catholicism*, trans. Lewis B. Smedes (Grand Rapids: William B. Eerdmans Publishing Company, 1965), 235.

12. Ott, 215.

13. Not only does the church's view of Mary as mediatrix and dispensatrix of all graces detract from Christ's role as our great High Priest, it also detracts from (at times almost replaces) the ministry of the Holy Spirit. We've already seen several examples from official teaching. Consider also the following quotation from Unger in his notes to *Ad Diem Illum* (p. 20): "As Mediator, Jesus Christ has a threefold office. He is King, Teacher and Priest. Mary, as Mediatrix, shares in this threefold office. She is Queen, Teacher and Sanctifier; she rules over us, teaches and sanctifies us." The reader should contrast such teachings of the church with the following Scriptures: John 14:26; Romans 8:26–27; 1 Corinthians 12:4–11; Ephesians 2:18 (which shows that the Holy Spirit, not Mary, serves as medium between the believer and Jesus Christ); 2 Thessalonians 2:13.

14. Quoted in Michael O'Carroll, *Theotokos: A Theological Encyclopedia of the Blessed Virgin Mary* (Wilmington, Del.: Michael Glazier, 1982), s.v. "Mediation, Mary Mediatress."

15. F. J. Sheed, *Theology for Beginners*, 3d ed. (Ann Arbor, Mich.: Servant Books, 1958), 132–33.

16. John Paul II, *Mother of the Redeemer* (encyclical letter *Redemptoris Mater*), Vatican trans. (Boston: Daughters of St. Paul, 1987), 56.

17. It must be noted that the larger issue here is the differing views held by Catholics and Protestants on justification. For a discussion of this, see Mitchell Pacwa and Walter Martin, "Justification by Faith: A Catholic-Protestant Dialogue," *Christian Research Journal*, Winter/Spring 1987, 24–27.

18. *Novena Prayers in Honor of Our Mother of Perpetual Help* (Uniontown, Pa.: Sisters of St. Basil, 1968), 19.

19. Austin Flannery, ed., *Vatican Council II: The Conciliar and Post Conciliar Documents* (Northport, N.Y.: Costello Publishing Company, 1975), 419.

20. St. Alphonsus de Liguori, *The Glories of Mary*, ed. Eugene Grimm (Brooklyn: Redemptorist Fathers, 1931), 83.

21. *Ibid.* 94.

22. *Ibid.*, 169.

23. *Ibid.*, 180–82.

24. *Ibid.*, 195–96.

25. *Ibid.*, 198.

26. *Ibid.*, 136–37.

27. *Ibid.*, 137.

28. *Ibid.*, 124

29. *Ibid.*, 273.

30. That the church's focus was originally centered entirely on Christ is not denied by Catholics, but is viewed in light of the doctrine that the Holy Spirit has led the church into a fuller understanding of revealed truth (e.g., Marian dogma) throughout the centuries. For example, in an effort to excuse the third-century theologian Origen for holding that Mary had been guilty of sin, one Mariologist writes: "We should not be astonished at these statements of Origen's, still less be scandalized; they must be 'excused,' let us say, by being set in their proper historical context. At a period when Christian devotion was centered entirely on Christ, it seemed to be the accepted thing to oppose the absolutely perfect holiness of the Lord with the sinful condition of all the redeemed" (Lucien Deiss, *Mary, Daughter of Sion*, trans. Barbara T. Blair [Collegeville, Minn.: The Liturgical Press, 1972], 211).

Chapter 7: Queen of Heaven

1. Pope Pius X, *Mary Mediatrix* (encyclical letter *Ad Diem Illum*), translated and annotated by Dominic J. Unger (Paterson, N.J.: St. Anthony Guild Press, 1948), 10.

2. Ludwig Ott, *Fundamentals of Catholic Dogma*, 4th ed., ed. in English by James Canon Bastible, D.D., trans. from the German by Patrick Lynch, Ph.D. (Rockford, Ill.: TAN Books and Publishers, 1974), 211.

3. Quoted in Eamon R. Carroll, "Mary in the Documents of the Magisterium," in *Mariology*, Vol. 1, ed. Juniper B. Carol (Milwaukee: Bruce Publishing Company, 1955), 49.

4. *Ibid.*, 45.

5. It might be asserted that this line of reasoning would necessitate that Christ also was exalted to deity by his followers, according to the same pattern. However, from the very beginning, Christ identified himself as God (e.g. John 8:58), and his followers worshiped him as such (e.g., Matt. 28:17). In the case of Mary, we do not find her later exaltation supported by early history.

6. Victor Buksbazen, *Miriam, the Virgin of Nazareth* (Philadelphia: Spearhead Press, 1963), 180–81.

7. Karl Keating, *Catholicism and Fundamentalism: The Attack on "Romanism" by "Bible Christians"* (San Francisco: Ignatius Press, 1988), 280.

8. For more on this, see J. N. D. Kelly, *Early Christian Doctrines* (New York: Harper and Row Publishers), ch. 18.

9. See, e.g., Kenneth Scott Latourette, *A History of Christianity*, vol. 1, *Beginnings to 1500*, rev. ed. (New York: Harper and Row Publishers, 1975), 209; Williston Walker, *A History of the Christian Church*, 3d ed. (New York: Charles Scribner's Sons, 1970), 156; Phillip Schaff, *History of the Christian Church*, Vol. 1 (N.p., AP&A, n.d.), 172–73; Tim Dowley, ed., *Eerdmans Handbook to the History of Christianity* (Grand Rapids: Eerdmans, 1977), 132, 296; and Arnold Toynbee, *Surviving the Future* (New York: Oxford University Press, 1971), 12.

Chapter 8: Hyperveneration

1. Ludwig Ott, *Fundamentals of Catholic Dogma*, 4th ed., ed. in English by James Canon Bastible, trans. from the German by Patrick Lynch (Rockford, Ill.: TAN Books and Publishers, 1974), 215.

2. Donald Grey Barnhouse, "The Origin of Mary Worship," *Eternity*, Aug. 1950, 23.

3. Quoted in Xavier Range, *Vatican Council II* (New York: Farrar, Straus and Giroux, 1968), 160.

4. *Ibid.*, 161.

5. Thomas Howard, *Evangelical Is Not Enough: Worship of God in Liturgy and Sacrament* (San Francisco: Ignatius Press, 1984), 89.

6. Some Catholics claim they do not pray *to* Mary, but only ask her to pray *for* them. However, even by the Catholic definition of the term, this is still prayer. And, as we saw in chapter 7, the fact is that most Catholic prayers to Mary are thorough-going prayers and not mere "prayer requests addressed to a Christian friend."

7. G. C. Berkouwer, *The Second Vatican Council and the New Catholicism*, trans. Lewis B. Smedes (Grand Rapids: William B. Eerdmans Publishing Company, 1965), 224.

8. *Ibid.*

9. See the two-part series, "The Modern World of Witchcraft" by Craig S. Hawkins in the Winter/Spring and Summer 1990 issues of *Christian Research Journal.*

Chapter 9: What Is an Apparition?

1. Rene Laurentin, quoted in Jeffery L. Sheler, "What's in a Vision?" *U.S. News & World Report*, 12 Mar. 1990, 67.

2. *Dictionary of Mary* (New York: Catholic Book Publishing Company, 1985), s.v. "Apparitions," 25–26.

3. Donald Attwater, ed., *A Catholic Dictionary* (New York: The Macmillan Company, 1961), s.v. "Apparition," 30.

4. *The Encyclopedia of Religion*, s.v. "Visions."

5. *Dictionary of Mary*, 25–26.

6. Kenneth Woodward, "Visitations of the Virgin," *Newsweek*, 20 July 1987, 54–55.

7. Sheler, 67.

8. Catherine M. Odell, *Those Who Saw Her: The Apparitions of Mary* (Huntington, Ind.: Our Sunday Visitor Publishing Division, 1986), 30.

9. Charlotte Low, "The Madonna's Decline and Revival," *Insight*, 9 Mar. 1990, 61.

Chapter 10: The Catholic Church's Evaluation

1. Louis Lochet, *Apparitions of Our Lady* (New York: Herder and Herder Publishing, 1960), 30.

2. *Dictionary of Mary* (New York: Catholic Book Publishing Company, 1985), s.v. "Apparitions," 26.

3. Rene Laurentin, cited in Catherine M. Odell, *Those Who Saw Her: The Apparitions of Mary* (Huntington, Ind.: Our Sunday Visitor Publishing Division, 1986), 27.

4. *Ibid.*, 19.

5. Mark Miravalle, *The Message of Medjugorje: The Marian Message to the Modern World* (New York: University Press of America, 1986), 103.

6. Jeffery L. Sheler, "What's in a Vision?" *U.S. News & World Report*, 12 Mar. 1990, 67.

Chapter 11: A Survey of Marian Apparitions

1. *New Catholic Encyclopedia* (New York: McGraw-Hill, 1967), s.v. "Guadalupe, Our Lady of."

2. *Ibid.*

3. *Dictionary of Mary* (New York: Catholic Book Publishing Company, 1985), s.v. "Apparitions," 110.

4. *New Catholic Encyclopedia*, s.v. "Lourdes," 1031.

5. *The Appearance of the Blessed Virgin Mary at the Grotto of Lourdes*, trans. J. B. Estrade and J. H. Girolestone (Westminster: Art and Book Co., 1912), 51, as cited in Mark Miravalle, *The Message of Medjugorje: The Marian Message to the Modern World* (New York: University Press of America, 1986), 104.

6. *Ibid.*, 109.

7. As cited in Miravelle, 108.

8. *New Catholic Encyclopedia*, s.v. "Lourdes."

9. Miravalle, 103.

10. *New Catholic Encyclopedia*, s.v. "Lourdes."

11. Ruth Cranston, *The Miracles of Lourdes* (New York: Image Book Doubleday, 1988), 339–51.

12. "Have Faith, Save Water," *Time*, 1 Oct. 1990, 67.

13. *New Catholic Encyclopedia*, s.v. "Fatima."

14. As cited in Miravalle, 112–13.

15. *Ibid.*, 114

16. *New Catholic Encyclopedia*, s.v. "Fatima," 855.

17. Gary DeMar, "An Appetite for Apocalypse," *The Biblical Worldview*, Oct. 1991, 5–8.

18. *Dictionary of Mary*, 32–33.

19. J. Gordon Melton, ed., *The Encyclopedia of American Religions* (Detroit: Gale Research 1989), 207.

20. *Ibid.*

Chapter 12: The Mystery of Medjugorje

1. The word *Medjugorje* is Croatian for "among the hills."

2. These figures were given to me by Catholic journalist Gabriel Meyer. He is based in Medjugorje and writes for the *National Catholic Register* and *Catholic Twin Circle*.

3. For extensive background information on the apparitions see: Rene Laurentin and Ljudevit Rupcic, *Is the Virgin Mary Appearing At Medjugorje?* trans. Francis Martin (Gaithersburg, Md.: The Word Among Us Press, 1984), and Rene Laurentin and Rene Lejeune, *Messages and Teachings of Mary at Medjugorje,* trans. Juan Gonzales, Jr. (Milford, Ohio: The Riehle Foundation, 1988).

4. As cited in Gabriel Meyer, *A Portrait of Medjugorje* (Studio City, Calif.: Twin Circle Publishing Company, 1990), 19.

5. As cited in Mary Craig, *Spark from Heaven: The Mystery of the Madonna of Medjugorje* (Notre Dame, Ind.: Ave Maria Press, 1988), 16. This quotation comes from an interview transcript for the BBC Everyman/Westernhanger film, *The Madonna of Medjugorje.*

6. Svetozar Kraljevic, *The Apparitions of Our Lady at Medjugorje: An Historical Account with Interviews,* ed. Michael Scanlan (Chicago: Franciscan Herald Press, 1984), 13.

7. *Ibid.*

8. As cited in Laurentin and LeJeune, 150.

9. Laurentin and Rupcic, 26–27.

10. Meyer, 23.

11. Laurentin and Rupcic, 31–32.

12. Mark Miravalle, *Heart of the Message of Medjugorje* (Steubenville, Ohio: Franciscan University Press, 1988), 14–16.

13. *Ibid.*, 30.

14. Rene Laurentin, *Latest News of Medjugorje (June 1987),* trans. Judith Lohre Stiens (Milford, Ohio: The Riehle Foundation, 1987), X.

15. See Edgar L. Havaich, "On a Hill Far Away: The Message and Miracles of Medjugorje," *The Quarterly Journal,* July/ September 1990, 5–7.

16. Rene Laurentin and Henri Joyeux, *Scientific and Medical Studies on the Apparitions at Medjugorje,* trans. Luke Griffin (Dublin: Veritas Publications, 1987).

17. Pavao Zanic, Bishop, *The Truth About Medjugorje* (unpublished manuscript, 1990), 15.

18. As cited in E. Michael Jones, "Medjugorje Goes Up in Smoke: The Yugoslavian Bishops Just Say No," *Fidelity,* February 1991, 16.

19. Chuck Sudetic, "Heavenly Visions? Bishop Says No," *New York Times,* 28 September 1990, A9.

20. Meyer, 27–28.

21. As cited in Jones, 16.

22. Meyer, 25.

Chapter 13: How Apparitions Have Influenced Catholic Piety

1. *New Catholic Encyclopedia* (New York: McGraw-Hill, 1967), s.v. "Rosary."

2. *Ibid.,* 667.

3. *Ibid.,* 668.

4. *Ibid.*

5. As cited in Mark Miravalle, *Heart of the Message of Medjugorje* (Steubenville, Ohio: Franciscan University Press, 1988), 52.

6. *Ibid.*

7. *New Catholic Encyclopedia,* s.v. "Rosary," 669.

8. *Ibid.,* s.v. "Scapulars."

9. *Ibid.,* 1115.

Chapter 14: A Protestant Evangelical Response

1. See Elliot Miller, "The Christian and Authority" (two parts), *Forward,* Spring 1985, 8–15; Summer 1985, 8–11, 2426; Kenneth R. Samples, "Does the Bible Teach 'Sola Scriptura'?" *Christian Research Journal,* Fall 1989, 31.

2. Geoffrey W. Bromiley, ed., *The International Standard Bible Encyclopedia* (Grand Rapids: William B. Eerdmans Publishing Company, 1978), s.v. "Mary."

3. See George Carey, *A Tale of Two Churches* (Downers Grove, Ill.: InterVarsity Press, 1985), 37.

4. Jaroslav Pelikan, *The Riddle of Roman Catholicism* (New York: Abingdon Press, 1960), 137.

5. Rene Laurentin, *Latest News of Medjugorje (June 1987),* trans. Judith Lohre Stiens (Milford, Ohio: The Riehle Foundation, 1987), 25–31.

6. Jan Connell, *Queen of the Cosmos: Interviews with the Visionaries* (Orleans, Mass.: Paraclete Press, 1990), 40.

7. For a detailed discussion of how counterfeit miracles (demonic) differ from true miracles (divine), consult Norman L. Geisler, *Signs and Wonders* (Wheaton, Ill.: Tyndale House Publishers, 1988).

8. Pelikan, 140.

Glossary

apocrypha As used in this book, synonymous with *pseudepigrapha* ("falsely ascribed"): Christian writings of questionable authorship and authenticity, written during the first five centuries A.D. Distinguished from *Christian Apocrypha* (capitalized): various early writings (usually authentic) which were proposed for inclusion in the New Testament but ultimately rejected by the major canons.

asceticism The pursuit of spiritual and eternal ends through severe physical and temporal self-deprivation.

apparition The sudden appearance of a supernatural entity which directly manifests itself to a human individual or group (a supernatural vision).

Deposit of the Faith, The In Catholic theology, the entire content of specially revealed truth, "deposited" by Christ to his apostles, completed with the death of the last surviving apostle, contained in Scripture and church tradition, and preserved and infallibly interpreted by the *magisterium* or teaching authority of the church.

ecumenism A movement devoted to promoting worldwide Christian unity through increased understanding and cooperation.

encyclical A letter of instruction from the pope which circulates throughout the church.

hyperveneration As understood and practiced in Catholicism, the expression of profound esteem, love, and devotion toward the Virgin Mary.

Immaculate Heart of Mary A symbol both of Mary's maternal love for humanity and of her total commitment to God.

indulgence The partial or complete remission of the penalties still due to be paid for sins which have already been forgiven in the sacrament of penance.

Marian dogma A belief concerning the Virgin Mary which is proposed by the Catholic church as an article of divine revelation.

Mariology (1) The totality of Catholic dogmas, beliefs, and speculations regarding Mary, the mother of Jesus. (2) That branch of Catholic theology concerned with the study of Marian doctrines.

monasticism An organized system of asceticism based on communal living in retreat from worldly involvements.

papal bull An official document, edict, or decree from the pope.

pious belief A belief that is recognized by the church as being in harmony with Catholic teaching.

priest In the biblical sense, a man divinely chosen and consecrated to represent men and women before God through offering sacrifices and making intercession.

purgatory In Catholic theology, a state of purification and/or maturation one may experience after death for the purpose of preparing one's soul to enter the presence of God.

veneration As understood and practiced in Catholicism, the expression of profound esteem and love toward one of the saints in heaven.

worship The expression of profound esteem, love, devotion, and adoration toward a deity or other revered object.

Appendix A

Medjugorje Up Close: Interviews with Key People Surrounding the Apparitions

Medjugorje is truly an unusual and complex phenomenon. In an attempt to get at the facts first hand, Kenneth R. Samples visited Medjugorje, Yugoslavia, in September 1990. During his visit he interviewed many key people connected to the apparitions (including all four of the youths who are still experiencing the visions). The following are transcripts of some of those interviews.

Interview with Visionary Vicka Ivankovic

Vicka: (b. July 3, 1964) is the most outspoken of the young visionaries. She talked with Kenneth Samples through an interpreter on September 15, 1990, at her home in the village of Medjugorje.

Kenneth: Vicka, for the most part, Protestants do not have devotion to Mary. So if some of my questions seem inappropriate or offensive, I apologize.

Vicka: No, please go ahead.

Kenneth: What makes you certain that the apparition is Mary, the mother of Jesus?

Vicka: I am sure, because the Virgin told me that she is the Blessed Virgin. I am also sure because we can see her as a live person, just as we can see you.

Kenneth: Has the apparition said anything about the truth or falsity of other religions?

Vicka: She has not said anything about other religions. But God said that he has not divided the religions; it is man who has divided the religions. But each man must respect his own religion, because there is only one God, and all of us are praying to the same God.

Kenneth: If the Catholic church does not approve these occurrences as authentic or genuine, how will that affect your understanding of these experiences?

Vicka: The Blessed Virgin has told us that we need not worry about that. She said that we should merely live her messages and that she would take care of everything.

Kenneth: Vicka, do you actually leave your body when you experience these apparitions?

Vicka: What do you mean?

Kenneth: Well, does your soul leave your body?

Vicka: All I can say is that during the apparitions I feel an indescribable joy. It is not like ecstasy. We all just feel great joy.

Kenneth: I was told that the apparition recommended a book by Maria Valtorta entitled *The Poem of the Man-God.*

Vicka: Marija asked the Virgin about that book, and the Virgin said that she should read that book, because it is like a poem between God and man.

Kenneth: Were you given special knowledge about Mary's early life? And if so, what has come of this information?

Vicka: I have three notebooks of recorded material about the Virgin's life. I am just waiting for the time when the Virgin will have me reveal it to others. Everything is ready; I'm just waiting for the right time.

Kenneth: Do you receive visions in your home or just at the church?

Vicka: It depends. For I was sick for a long time and so I stayed at home, but now I go to the church. So it depends, sometimes at home, and sometimes at church.

Kenneth: Do all of the visionaries see the apparitions the same way, or is it individual?

Vicka: All of us have the vision at the same time. And we all see it the same way and get the same message.

Kenneth: Vicka, thank you for speaking with us. You are very kind.

Vicka: Thank you. You are welcome.

Interview with the "Seventh Visionary," Jelena Vasilj

Jelena Vasilj (18 years old at the time of the interview) has been called the seventh visionary. She claims that she has been receiving messages from the Virgin Mary since December 15, 1982. However, Jelena's experiences have been called inner locutions: She reports that she hears Mary within her heart or soul during times of deep meditative prayer. Her alleged encounters with Mary are not external, three-dimensional visions like those claimed by the other six visionaries.

Like Vicka, Jelena spoke with Kenneth Samples through an interpreter at her home in Medjugorje. Also participating in the September 16, 1990, interview was Paul Carden, a research consultant at the Christian Research Institute.

Kenneth: Were you troubled when you first began receiving these messages?

Jelena: Yes, because in the beginning I didn't know who it was that was speaking to me.

Kenneth: When this began, did you try in any way to test these experiences? How do you know that it is Mary that is speaking?

Jelena: I was only ten years old when this began. So I didn't attempt to test anything.

Kenneth: So, then, what makes you certain that this is Mary speaking?

Jelena: In the beginning I felt an inner security. Also, later the Blessed Virgin introduced herself and I felt a great peace.

Kenneth: Has anyone representing the Catholic church or connected to the church's commission to investigate these occurrences spoken with you?

Jelena: A couple of years ago a member of the commission spoke with me.

Kenneth: Did you take part in the medical examinations that the other visionaries underwent?

Jelena: No.

Paul: Has anyone expressed interest in doing that someday?

Jelena: I don't know anything about anyone wanting to do an exam. Probably you do not know the kind of gift I have. Because my gift is an inner experience, I'm not sure anyone could conduct an exam. Maybe just a psychological exam.

Paul: Have you had psychological exams?

Jelena: No.

Kenneth: Do you know the other visionaries?

Jelena: If you know them, then you know that I know them, because we live in the same village. Most everybody knows each other.

Kenneth: Are you close friends?

Jelena: We are not close friends.

Kenneth: Do the visionaries accept the messages you receive?

Jelena: They have never said anything about me, and I have never asked them. I never had a reason to ask them.

Kenneth: Have you been told anything about the truth or falsity of other religions?

Jelena: The Blessed Virgin has said nothing about other religions. Vicka told me that God has not divided the religions. I do not know what many people believe in their different faiths in God. The Blessed Virgin has told me that she is the mother of everybody.

Kenneth: Do you have an opinion about the other visionaries? Do you feel strongly in favor of their visions?

Jelena: I was very young when the visions started and so I didn't think much about it. I just accepted the messages, but I had a feeling that they were true. Even now I have that feeling.

Kenneth: If the Catholic church rejects your experiences and that of the other visionaries, how would that affect your understanding of these events?

Jelena: If the church said that these things going on in Medjugorje are not true it would not change my life, because I am sure about what's going on. So it will not change my life. But I have heard the pope say that it is true because of how it makes the people's faith stronger.

Kenneth: Is it difficult dealing with all of these people?

Jelena: Finding the time is sometimes difficult, because I must find time for work, for school, for family, and for the groups. So it is only the time that is difficult.

Kenneth: Do you have a priest who counsels with you or gives you guidance on a regular basis?

Jelena: More or less through confession.

Kenneth: Before you began having these experiences, were you a strong Catholic believer? How has your spiritual life changed?

Jelena: I went to church with my family. I didn't feel any special need for the church, probably because I was only ten years old. But now I feel stronger because I feel a need for God.

Kenneth: Has your family been involved with other religions besides Catholicism?

Jelena: No.

Paul: Has anyone in the church questioned your messages?

Jelena: The church has said nothing, neither yes nor no.

Kenneth: Do you know when the messages will cease?

Jelena: I do not know. It has lasted a long time. I can only guess.

Kenneth: Have you experienced any special miracles?

Jelena: I have never experienced any physical healing.

Kenneth: Are you encouraged to read the Bible and to recite the creed?

Jelena: Yes, both of them.

Interview with Visionary Marija Pavlovic

Marija (b. April 1, 1964) is probably the most reflective of the visionaries. She spoke with Kenneth Samples after an evening apparition at St. James Parish, September 19, 1990.

Kenneth: Marija, what makes you certain that the apparition is in fact Mary, the mother of Jesus Christ?

Marija: The apparition itself. I see her and speak to her, just as I speak to you.

Kenneth: If the Catholic church does not approve of these apparitions, how will that affect your understanding of these events?

Marija: What the church does is not my concern. My concern is to live the messages that the Blessed Mother has given.

Kenneth: Does it bother you that the bishop is so vehemently opposed to the apparitions?

Marija: I simply love and pray for the bishop.

Kenneth: Do you know when the apparitions will cease?

Marija: No, I do not.

Kenneth: Has the apparition said anything about the truth or falsity of other religions?

Marija: The Blessed Mother has told us that there is only one God and that we should respect other religions.

Interview with Visionary Ivan Dragicevic

Ivan (b. May 25, 1965) is the oldest male visionary. He spoke with Kenneth Samples on September 14, 1990, at his home in

Medjugorje. Because of its considerable length, this dialogue has been abbreviated.

Kenneth: Has the apparition communicated anything concerning the truth or falsity of other religions?

Ivan: Our Lady, when she came, didn't say anything particular about this. When she arrived, she arrived with a message for the whole world and for those who want to live the messages. Those messages are directed toward peace and conversion; not conversion in the sense that someone is to transfer himself under Catholicism, but to come back to the gospel: to leave sin and obey the commandments. I am not able to comment on any other direction or sects. My personal opinion is that we are dividing ourselves too much in that way, and we are forgetting God.

Kenneth: What makes you certain that the apparition is in fact Mary, the mother of Jesus? Is there a criterion?

Ivan: What I can say is that when Our Lady arrived she said that she was sent by her Son. In the first day of the apparitions she announced the main messages. We were not certain in the first few days that it was Our Lady. The second day when we arrived there was me, Jacov, Vicka, Ivanka, and Mirjana. Vicka's grandmother gave some holy water to them and told them to make the sign of the cross with the holy water in front of the apparition; if it is not really Our Lady she will fade. But Our Lady only smiled and she remained. After that she introduced herself as the holy Virgin Mary, with the subtitle of Queen of Peace. We see Our Lady in three dimensions, which means that we can see her just as I can see you now. And I speak to her as I am speaking to you now. And I can say after nine years of the apparitions of Our Lady, that I feel more relaxed with her than with you now. I can also touch her. If what I see were not so certain I wouldn't have made such a sacrifice as I've made all these nine years. If what I'm seeing were not true, I would have gone another way. It was enough to have five years of different kinds of research conducted—medical and theoretical, but especially medical—in which we went through everything. I don't believe there is anything we didn't go through. There came the most skillful and competent experts in this area, especially medical.

Kenneth: What was the basic conclusion of the doctors who gave the exams?

Ivan: I can't say what the whole conclusions were on the basis of everything, but I can say that all those terms like *hallucinations* were considered, and it was concluded that they were not present.

Kenneth: If the Catholic church does not officially accept these apparitions, how will this affect your understanding of these events?

Ivan: My personal opinions about these experiences will never change under any condition. And I'm not making myself worry about such things.

Kenneth: Do you leave your body when you experience an apparition? Is this an out-of-body experience?

Ivan: The time of the apparition is a time of ecstasy where everything else disappears and we have total concentration toward Our Lady. I experience no outside or external stimuli.

Kenneth: Can the apparitions appear any time? I know that they appear each evening at twenty minutes to seven. But can they occur any time, anywhere?

Ivan: From the first days of the apparitions, Our Lady appeared about twenty minutes until seven. So the time has remained firm throughout all these years. We start preparing for the apparition about six o'clock. We prepare ourselves for the apparition and the mass that follows by praying the rosary and other prayers. I see no reason for this event to happen at any other time.

Kenneth: Could you describe your spiritual commitment before the apparitions began? Were you a strong Catholic believer?

Ivan: The difference between my faith these years and the time before is very big, showing great change. My faith was real but superficial before: I was praying on the surface. It was not as deep as it should be, as it is becoming now. I can say that I now have in my life stability, assurance, and peace. This helps me in what I am doing.

Kenneth: Do all the visionaries come away with the same perception of the apparition, or is it individual?

Ivan: We all *see* the same, but we *experience* everything individually. And when the Blessed Mother says something to one of us, only that one person experiences it. But if something is for everyone, then everybody experiences it.

Kenneth: Does the apparition have prior knowledge about your lives—a knowledge of things that you have not communicated?

Ivan: Life wouldn't be interesting if we knew what was going to happen, and definitely she knows that. But when something bad is going to happen she tries to warn us about it. However, what is going to happen is going to happen. Our Lady best knows what we think.

Kenneth: Does the apparition speak much about the person of Jesus? Are these messages Christ centered?

Ivan: Of course. Most of the messages that Our Lady is giving are the messages of her Son. Some people are saying that Catholic people put Our Lady in front of Jesus. I wouldn't agree with that. It is a fact that she is here. But we do not neglect Jesus. We pray to Our Lady *and* to Jesus.

Interview with Bishop Pavao Zanic

Bishop Zanic, whose diocese includes Medjugorje, led the initial commission which investigated the apparitions. He is absolutely opposed to the events in Medjugorje. He spoke with Kenneth Samples through an interpreter at his office in Mostar, Yugoslavia on September 17, 1990. Because of its considerable length, this transcript has been abbreviated.

Kenneth: Bishop Zanic, I have come to Medjugorje to investigate the so-called apparitions. I believe it is important for me to speak with you if I am going to understand this complex phenomenon. I know that you are convinced that the apparitions in Medjugorje are fraudulent. However, I would like to ask you some questions.

Bishop: Please.

Kenneth: If the evidence against Medjugorje was strong and substantial in the first commission which you headed, why a second commission?

Bishop: I don't know.

Kenneth: Who decided that the second commission was necessary?

Bishop: The Congregation for the Faith. Five or six years before the apparitions began, the Congregation made out certain rules to govern the research. These said that if the bishop's commission does not reach a certain conclusion, and if the phenomenon rises up more than it should, then the whole process is to go to the Commission of the Bishop's Conference. And if it is necessary then it will go to a third commission, which would be international. For the third commission there would be a necessary transferring of books and things.

Kenneth: So the calling of the second commission was merely normal procedure, not a criticism of you and your initial commission.

Bishop: In the world it was understood as if the Holy Father had rejected me and my commission. But those in Rome haven't even asked to see what the commission was working on.

Kenneth: So you have not received criticism from anyone in Rome about your commission.

Bishop: No. On the contrary, I have had good things said about it.

Kenneth: How did your initial commission vote regarding Medjugorje?

Bishop: Two friars voted that the supernatural had been confirmed. One said that maybe something supernatural happened in the beginning. One didn't want to vote. And eleven persons voted that they found nothing supernatural.

Kenneth: You say in your booklet that the vast majority of priests and bishops in Yugoslavia reject the apparitions in Medjugorje. Is it then probable that the second commission will agree with your initial commission?

Bishop: I hope that no one on the commission will say that there is something supernatural going on there. There is a line of thinking and opinion prevailing that we should not say whether it is appearing or not appearing, but simply let the people come and pray. This is dangerous, because the faith of the people will be based on untruth.

Kenneth: Do you believe that the seers have put their visions above the authority of the church?

Bishop: For sure. They do not listen to the bishop.

Kenneth: If the church fails to give its approval, what should be the proper response on the part of the pilgrims who visit Medjugorje?

Bishop: It is very hard when obedience is lost. The church said that there was nothing supernatural about the apparitions in Garabandal, Spain. But until now there are many pilgrims pushing to reach the place.

Kenneth: Are the priests who have come out in support of Medjugorje being presumptuous in that they have not yet heard the official word from the church?

Bishop: They know that I do not approve of it. They are attacking me terribly. Look at how far this naive thing has gone. There is a place in Austria where a chemical herbicide created a cross-like shape in the grass of someone's garden. People claimed that it was from heaven and supernatural. The local bishop investigated and found nothing supernatural. Nevertheless, ten years later the family who owns the garden still lives well from the many pilgrims.

Kenneth: Did your commission find any evidence of the occult?

Bishop: What is happening in these places can be supernatural, or parapsychological, or someone simply making up an untruth. It is very hard to say what it is. I am sure that it is not supernatural.

Kenneth: But your commission found no evidence of the occult.

Bishop: No.

Kenneth: Is there any evidence to support the so-called miracles which are claimed to have taken place in Medjugorje—things like solar miracles, crosses spinning, and rosaries turning to gold?

Bishop: Nothing!

Kenneth: How would you explain the so-called solar miracles? Are they merely psychological?

Bishop: Nothing! Once I heard that a miracle was to occur, so I took my camera and went to the hill and nothing happened. They said that that very day something happened. I saw nothing.

Kenneth: In your booklet, you wrote that Mirjana has stated that the apparition says that all faiths are equal.

Bishop: Our Lady cannot say that.

Kenneth: Does that trouble you?

Bishop: It convinces me that it is not Our Lady.

Kenneth: Some argue that that statement is not addressed to non-Christian religions, so it is not advocating pluralism. I believe that Laurentin argues this way.

Bishop: That is his personal understanding.

Kenneth: Do you think that the medical exams which were performed on the seers were adequate and reliable?

Bishop: No.

Kenneth: You say in your booklet that Vicka, Ivan, and Mirjana have lied to you. Do you have evidence of this? Tape recordings?

Bishop: I have tapes. There are also her written contradictions.

Kenneth: Are you writing a book on Medjugorje?

Bishop: I am very, very busy, so it is going slowly, but I am working on that.

Kenneth: Thank you for your frankness, your honesty, and your kindness.

Bishop: You are welcome.

Appendix B

A Catholic Scholar's Response to This Book

As was stated in the introduction, the underlying purpose of this book is ultimately ecumenical rather than antiecumenical: to promote open dialogue and understanding among Catholics and Protestants about an issue that continues to separate them. To better serve this purpose we asked Father Mitchell Pacwa, S.J., a Scripture scholar from Loyola University at Chicago, if we might include his thoughts and criticisms regarding our book within its pages. He graciously agreed to do so. Pacwa is an able scholar and apologist whose manner of life evidences a strong personal relationship with Christ. We have enjoyed with him the kind of relationship we advocate between Bible-believing Catholics and Protestants: honest and respectful discussion of our differences, but also positive fellowship in Christ and cooperative efforts in the common cause of Christ's kingdom. Pacwa's rebuttal follows.*

I appreciate this opportunity to offer my reflections on Ken Samples and Elliot Miller's book. These include an explanation of those aspects of Mariology that offend Protestant sensitivities. The main areas of difficulty are the basis for devotion to Mary (and the rest of the saints), the doctrines of Mary's immaculate conception and assumption, and the dangers of her taking precedence over Jesus Christ.

An anomaly appears in the claim that devotion to Mary was on the periphery of Christian life prior to the Council of Chalcedon (chapter 2), and yet the authors admit that the contrast between Mary and Eve in the mid-second century "was the actual beginning of what has developed into today's Mariology." The Council of Ephesus was held in a church dedicated to Mary, which indicates devotion was established and accepted in ancient times, well before Chalcedon.

Catholics have devotion to Mary and the saints because the Scriptures summon us to it. Hebrews 12:22–24 says: "But you have approached Mount Zion, the city of the living God, the heavenly Jerusalem, and myriads of angels, and the assembly and church of the firstborn who have been enrolled in heaven, and God the judge of all, and spirits of righteous ones who have been made perfect, and Jesus, mediator of a new covenant, and the sprinkled blood which speaks better than that of Abel." These "spirits of the righteous who have been made perfect" refers not to incarnate humans on earth but to those spirits of the just whom God has made perfect in heaven. Each Christian is summoned by Scripture to approach these saints, the "firstborn enrolled in heaven," as well as God the judge of all, Jesus the mediator, and the angels. A lack of devotion to the saints is unscriptural. Note also that the saints in heaven offer prayers to Jesus, including the offering of the prayers of the saints, presumably those still on earth, according to Revelation 4:10; 5:8; and 6:9–11.

At the same time, in no way does this subordinate Christ's uniquely salvific role as mediator. Only Jesus, as a true human entering into our sinful condition so that "for our sakes God made Him who did not know sin to become sin so that in Him we might become the very holiness of God" (2 Cor. 5:21), and truly God,

Appendix B

capable of being an infinite and eternal sacrifice for sin, is our redeemer. Pope Leo the Great (A.D. 449) stated the truth that Jesus is the one mediator, in his *Tome*, as did the Council of Trent (Session V, 1546). Vatican II's teaching on Mary makes explicit that Mary's intercession "in no way obscures or diminishes this unique mediation of Christ, but rather shows its power" (*Lumen Gentium*, no. 60).

Is there danger in this teaching? Yes, just as there is danger in any doctrine when it is taken out of context. We are all aware of heresy being taught in the name of biblical inerrancy, belief in Christ's healing power, charismatic gifts, and nearly every other biblical doctrine. However, we cannot let fear of error prevent us from proclaiming biblical doctrines. Rather, we who are teachers must do all we can to teach the gospel in all its fullness so as to maintain a true and biblically balanced faith.

The doctrines of the immaculate conception and the assumption remain as problems between Protestants and Catholics, but we Catholics believe them because of Scripture interpretation which antecedes Protestantism by centuries, not because we want to create doctrines. Sympathy with the Catholic approach to these doctrines will help Protestants see the insight they contain and open the way to a more fruitful discussion on these highly controversial topics.

Let us examine the immaculate conception. It would be helpful for the reader to appreciate that St. Augustine excepted the Virgin Mary from sin "for the sake of the honor of the Lord" (see Ott, *Fundamentals of Catholic Dogma*, p. 201). This was no desire to deify the Virgin Mary into a goddess but to recognize that Jesus, the new covenant, would be presented to the world in the pure and sinless ark of Mary's womb.

Admittedly, we differ in understanding Mary as one who is "full of grace," "graced," or "favored." However, I would at least want Protestants to understand that we Catholics have honestly accepted that this is a biblical basis for believing that the angelic greeting is so true that Mary's gracious state left no room for sin, including original sin.

Further biblical evidence comes when Elizabeth called Mary "blessed among women" (Luke 1:42), a Semitic way of saying, "You are the most blessed of all women." (Hebrew and Aramaic express the comparative and superlative with the preposition *from* and cannot add the equivalent of *-er* or *-est* to an adjective.) Mary is the most blessed woman, as Elizabeth proclaimed under the inspiration of the Holy Spirit, and for this reason "all generations will call [Mary] blessed" (Luke 1:48). Mary is, therefore, even more blessed than our mother, Eve, who was conceived without original sin, as all Christians believe. What makes Mary more blessed? Both the fact that she bore her Savior and that, unlike the immaculately conceived Eve, Mary was immaculately conceived and never sinned. Sinlessness is the only true blessing, and Mary is the most blessed woman who ever existed because, by God's grace, she never sinned.

The possibility of Christ preserving Mary from original sin is biblical, since Revelation 13:8 calls Christ "the Lamb who has been slain from the foundation of the world." His saving death since the foundation of the world is true because of his divinity. This eternal saving death makes possible Mary's immaculate conception; nothing in Mary made it possible for her to save herself from sin.

Chapter 4 fails to include two important elements regarding Mary's assumption. The first is Revelation 12, where the woman clothed in the sun, with the moon under her feet, and crowned with the twelve stars gives birth to the Messiah. Many theologians see this woman as the church, but that cannot be correct, since the church cannot give birth to Christ, but Christ gives birth to the church. Rather, this is Mary in her heavenly glory, since she (not the whole nation of Israel) gave birth to Christ. This forms part of the Catholic understanding of Mary's assumption. The second element is the biblical precedents for assumption into heaven: Enoch and Elijah. Since they were assumed into heaven even before the new covenant, because they were just, how much more proper would it be for Mary?

This book claims that "none of these dogmas are biblical" (p. 41), but Catholics claim they are biblical. A clearer statement of the situation would be that Protestants and Catholics approach the biblical materials in different ways. Catholic reflection on Scripture has drawn out logical conclusions about Mary. This applies not only to doctrines, such as the immaculate conception and assumption, but also to aspects of piety, such as seeing her as the mother of Jesus Christ, in whose mystical body we have been reborn.

Chapter 7, on the queenship of Mary says pagan ideas are the origin of her elevation as queen. The authors believe that a pagan need for divine queenship remained in the Christian church. However, this ignores the scriptural roots for her queenship in Catholic liturgy and practice, such as Psalm 45:11–16 or Revelation 12, where the woman clothed in the sun is crowned with the twelve stars, as if she were a queen, plus the role of the queen mother in ancient Israel.

These are logical developments of scriptural teaching in the same way that the definitions of the natures of Christ and the relations of the blessed trinity are logical developments, even though they are not explicitly taught by Scripture. The type of literalism of the Jehovah's Witnesses, rejecting the development of scriptural doctrine, would eliminate many teachings of tradition which Catholics and Protestants hold in common, though Scripture is not explicit on them.

I have already mentioned that Catholic doctrine does not allow us to replace Jesus with Mary or to see her intercession as superior to that of Jesus. He is the unique mediator, and her role adds nothing to and subtracts nothing from his saving role as God incarnate. The book expresses fear that the laity do not learn the subtle distinctions made by the theologians and therefore the Marian doctrines are not only wrong but dangerous. Evidence, even from

Catholic sources, is that in some cultures, especially the Latin countries, Mary has taken precedence over Christ.

All Christian doctrines are open to abuse. A couple once came to me for counsel. They admitted that they were committing adultery, but reasoned that since they had accepted Jesus and were saved, adultery must be God's will for them. That is a travesty of Protestant doctrine, which needs correction. So also, Catholic doctrines can be twisted out of recognition. Two antidotes are the liturgy and the Scriptures.

The Catholic liturgy celebrates various feasts of Mary throughout the year, but never do we pray to her in the church's official prayer. All prayers on Marian feast days are explicitly directed to God the Father, through Jesus his Son, in union with the Holy Spirit. Anyone can check a Catholic sacramentary for evidence. Also, the litanies of Mary (or the other saints) contain a key distinction about the kinds of intercession made by the faithful: petitions addressed to God the Father, Son, and Holy Spirit are "have mercy on us"; never is this addressed to Mary or the saints, who only get the intercession "pray for us." This distinction is heard and prayed and understood by the simplest peasant who says these approved prayers. A principle of theology called *lex orandi, lex credendi* (the rule of praying guides the rule of faith) teaches Catholics about the difference between the way God answers our prayers and has mercy on us, in distinction to Mary and the saints, who pray for us as fellow creatures.

A return to the reading of Scripture (which, contrary to popular Protestant opinion, has never been prohibited by the church), is the other antidote to misconceptions about Marian devotion. Marian devotions and books dependent upon private revelation or flowing from an individual's private mystical prayer often make me uncomfortable. I do not intend to say that all such private revelation is necessarily heretical, but I feel uncomfortable with it. This flourishes most at times when Scripture is ignored. I believe strongly and teach strenuously that healthy Marian devotion is tempered and enriched most by praying over the Scriptures. Asking the Holy Spirit who inspired the Word of God to inspire our understanding of it, we must listen to what God is saying to us.

Catholics and Protestants alike can search the Scriptures and pray over those passages where the blessed Mary appears: the incarnation of the Word of God, his sacred birth, his presentation at the temple—where Simeon tells Mary that a sword will pierce her heart so that the inner thoughts of many might be revealed (Luke 2:35), his being found in the temple (where the Bible says Jesus was obedient to Joseph and Mary), his first miracle at Cana, his death, and Pentecost. The Scriptures provide us with a rich feast in which we can learn more about this woman who still tells us to do whatever Jesus says. Further, we can understand these texts about Mary only in the context of the whole of the Scripture, not as something isolated from it. The church teaches us this in the liturgy of the hours and in the mass, and I only hope that all Catholics experience this richness of teaching about Mary and a sincere love and devotion to her.

The conclusion that "clear scriptural evidence" shows that Satan is behind Medjugorje (pp. 129–30) is too facile. Dr. Walter Martin (founder of the Christian Research Institute) was open to Medjugorje when he heard that the children were told to pray to Jesus rather than Mary, because she could not save them; Jesus is God, not she. Further, the message to repent and confess sin, to pray and believe the creed, does not seem demonic at all. A satanic origin for Medjugorje is too strong a conclusion.

Also, though Protestants disagree, Catholics base purgatory, penance, and veneration of the saints on Scripture; they are not cultic ideas. At worst, Medjugorje is a delusion, and the psychological aspects in the visionaries must be taken more seriously than the satanic. Remember, if the visionaries are partially or completely deluded, their background is still Catholic, which will strongly influence their understanding of the visions. Rather than satanic influence, see normal Catholic teaching as the reason for speaking of purgatory, devotion to Mary and the saints, and penance. A satanic explanation seems rather silly.

The claim that "receiving information from the dead . . . is entirely foreign to Scripture" (p. 133) is factually not true. Our Lord spoke with Moses and Elijah on the mountain, though they had died or been assumed centuries earlier. This is a solid Scriptural precedent for the kind of Marian apparitions of the last decades, especially if she, like Elijah, was assumed bodily into heaven.

While I personally withhold final judgment about Medjugorje, and I have some questions about it, too, I still would not conclude that it is satanic.

This book contains a number of other problems, some factual and some doctrinal. Correcting errors and difficulties regarding Mary's role on celibacy would take four more pages, which I do not have. In general, the first part of the book does not present as full an understanding of Marian theology in the Catholic church as I would like. The second part makes fair presentations of the stories of the various Marian apparitions, though I disagree strongly with the conclusions made about them.

Appendix C

The Authors' Reply to Father Pacwa

If more Catholics were as Christ-centered and biblically based in their thinking as is Father Mitchell Pacwa, the place of Mary in the Catholic church would be less troubling to Protestants. We wish him all the best in his efforts to correct extremes within the church through an emphasis on Scripture.

Certainly, we disagree with Pacwa as strongly as he does with us on many of the points he raises. But we also appreciate the theological perspective and historical context he has brought to this discussion. Our goal that the Catholic position be fairly represented in this book has been amply furthered by his contribution.

At many points the arguments he presents are sufficiently answered, we believe, within the main text of this book, and so it seems unnecessary to repeat ourselves here. We do feel the need, however, to briefly address some of the objections he raises.

As we affirmed in chapter 6, Catholic Mariology can be traced back to the mid-second century Eve–Mary typology. But the use of such typology does not indicate that a cult of devotion to Mary existed within the mainstream of the church, nor would its use have been sufficient to bring such a cult about. Chalcedon's proclamation that Mary is the mother of God was necessary to set the stage for that.

The fact that the church at Ephesus was dedicated to Mary does not go far in proving a widespread devotion to Mary before Chalcedon. It is widely noted that the cult of Mary appears at Ephesus at a comparatively early time. The city had been specially dedicated to the Greek goddess Artemis (Acts 19) until the end of the pagan era. It would appear that the void in popular religious devotion created by the banishment of Artemis was quickly filled by Mary (chapter 7).

Hebrews 12:22–24 does not *instruct* us to "come to" departed saints (in devotional prayer). It rather *informs* us that we "have come" (perfect tense) to these spirits. In other words, by identifying through faith with Christ we have also identified ourselves with all that is his. The passage also tells us we have approached the heavenly Jerusalem and myriads of angels. But though by faith we are citizens of the new Jerusalem and have joined the company of the angels, we have no present interaction with these heavenly realities. Neither do we have any present contact (i.e., through prayer) with the spirits of just men made perfect.

In chapter 6 we acknowledge that the Catholic church seeks to preserve the uniqueness of Christ's mediation. At the same time we argue that its efforts in this regard have failed to a significant degree: the church's teachings on and devotion to Mary undermine the integrity of Christ's high priesthood. Our arguments along these lines are not answered by Pacwa, nor do we believe they can be satisfactorily refuted.

We agree that biblical doctrines can be taken out of context and thus made the basis for abusive practice. The issue here is, Is religious devotion to anyone but God biblical? We believe we have shown that it is not. If it is not, then there is no way to practice it without some adverse effects resulting, although admittedly these can be tempered by efforts to maintain a perceived "biblical balance."

Although we suggest that an (often unconscious) urge to exalt Mary has historically been a driving force behind Catholic Mariology, we also acknowledge that other factors, such as a misplaced desire to protect Christ's divinity, have figured in (chapter 2). Augustine's teaching that Jesus needed to be presented to the world in the "pure and sinless ark of Mary's womb" is an example of this misplaced devotion to Christ. Our argument against the idea of Mary's perpetual virginity—that Jesus came to identify with sinners—is applicable to Augustine's view as well. Jesus' divinity would only be violated if it were held that he himself sinned or was born with original sin.

The assertion that "sinlessness is the only true blessing" must be challenged, for many in the Bible are called blessed who are nonetheless sinners (e.g., Matt. 5:3–11). Mary was truly blessed among women to be made the mother of our Savior, whether she was sinless or not.

We were aware that Catholic theologians had traditionally associated Revelation 12 with Mary, but our reading indicated that this interpretation is falling out of use. For example, G. C. Berkouwer (*The Second Vatican Council and the New Catholicism*, trans. Lewis B. Smedes [Grand Rapids: William B. Eerdmans Publishing Company, 1965], 229) observes:

> Pius IX's remark that "everyone knows" that Revelation 12:1 refers to Mary is not reflected in later Catholic exegesis. The awareness of the peculiar apocalyptic literary genre has led to more reservations about the references to Mary that people used to see in John's Revelation. Some Catholic exegetes baldly say that the Marian interpretation of this text is simply false. In his commentary on the book of Revelation, the Catholic exegete Wikenhauser flatly says that the Marian interpretation of Revelation 12:1 has been "abandoned by modern scientific exegesis."

This is why we did not deal with this proof text. However, at Pacwa's urging, we will deal with it here.

It is difficult to view the woman of Revelation 12 as Mary, since the events described there do not correspond with anything we know about her. There is no biblical or historical evidence that she was persecuted and fled into the wilderness after Christ's ascension into heaven. Even if we take this language symbolically, it is difficult to conceive what it might symbolize.

Furthermore, there is nothing in this passage that supports Mary's assumption. It is the woman's son who is assumed into heaven, while she remains on the earth. The text will not allow for Pacwa's interpretation that "this is Mary in her heavenly glory." Or are we to believe that Satan persecutes her in heaven?

That the events described occur on the earth creates another problem for the Marian interpretation. This is an eschatological passage relating to the final days of human history (vv. 10, 12). Clearly these events cannot be placed within the earthly lifetime of Mary.

While recognizing that even Protestants debate the meaning of this vision, we suggest that the woman represents faithful (as opposed to apostate) Israel throughout the centuries. It was from her "womb" that Christ came into the world. Having accepted Jesus as her Messiah (Rom. 11:25–32), she will be persecuted in the last days by the Antichrist, but protected by God. This view is strongly supported by the fact that the imagery used for the woman (the sun, the moon, and twelve stars) originally appears in a vision the patriarch Joseph had of his family, the nucleus of the nation Israel (Gen. 37:9–11).

Psalm 45:11–16 is very unconvincing as a proof text for Mary's queenship. The King (Jesus?) desires her beauty? Mary is not in that text unless one *puts* her there through an allegorical hermeneutic that must be considered arbitrary.

Protestants reject aspects of both the Catholic and Jehovah's Witness approaches to doctrinal development, viewing them as opposite extremes (though certainly the Catholic view is preferable to that of the Witnesses). We agree with Catholics that the Holy Spirit has been actively guiding the church into a deeper understanding of essential doctrine throughout its history (although we do not understand the *church* to be synonymous with *Roman Catholicism*). But there is no biblical basis for saying that the church is infallible. In fact, the Protestant Reformation can be viewed as an instance of the Holy Spirit instructing and correcting the church on matters such as justification and authority.

We further agree with Catholics that some biblical doctrines are taught implicitly rather than explicitly, and therefore some reflection is required to identify them. But we contend that many Catholic doctrines, including several Marian beliefs, are not even implicitly present in Scripture. They were derived from traditional and popular sources and then read into, not drawn out of, Scripture.

The key to determining what is and is not a biblical doctrine is found in allowing Scripture to interpret itself, rather than imposing an external interpretive system on it (which is how we would characterize the allegorical method of hermeneutics). This is done (among other things) by carefully considering its historical and grammatical context, and by understanding its meaning as literal except when a different interpretation can be justified by the immediate and larger context of Scripture itself.

Unfortunately, Pacwa came away with the impression that we definitely conclude that Satan is behind Medjugorje. Rather, what we say is that the origin or cause of Marian apparitions (Medjugorje included) must be either natural or supernatural. We then conclude that *if* the cause is supernatural *then* we can only be dealing with the demonic, and not with God, because of the unbiblical nature of Marian apparitions. This conclusion does not preclude a naturalistic explanation of Marian apparitions such as Medjugorje. But, as we state, we do believe that there is good reason to seriously consider a demonic interpretation of these unusual occurrences, especially in Medjugorje.

Pacwa, on the other hand, states that to entertain a satanic interpretation of Medjugorje is facile and even silly. However, Pacwa's quick dismissal of the demonic strikes us as a bit undiscerning for three reasons. First, these events are incredibly elusive. Since not even the Catholic church can guarantee their authenticity, no explanation should be quickly ruled out. Second, even some Catholic scholars have suspected a demonic influence behind Medjugorje. Third, given our Protestant convictions (particularly our rejection of most of Catholic Mariology), our belief in the devil, Medjugorje's alleged supernatural manifestations, its possible occultic aspects, and the seeming honesty and psychological soundness of its visionaries, it is logically consistent for us to entertain a demonic explanation. Is it silly to hold that Satan can manifest himself to human beings under a benign disguise? Secular humanists might say so, but Pacwa, who believes in the Bible, should not (2 Cor. 11:14).

Pacwa cites the appearance of Moses and Elijah to Jesus on the mount of transfiguration (Matt. 17:1–13; Mark 9:2–13; Luke 9:28–36) as a biblical precedent for apparitions. However, the two phenomena are quite different. The purpose of the transfiguration (preview of Christ's glory) was to give confirmation of Jesus' messianic fulfillment of both the law (Moses) and the prophets (Elijah). This occurrence was a unique event in the life and ministry of Jesus Christ. In no way does it sanction the appearance of other departed saints to ordinary believers to give them prophetic instruction and information, a phenomenon which *is* "entirely foreign to Scripture."

We should add that while Walter Martin was surprised by the seeming Christocentric message of Medjugorje, in the final analysis he considered Marian apparitions to be an unbiblical phenomenon.

Postscript on Medjugorje

While the authors have endeavored to insure that the information given in this book is as accurate and current as possible, recent events in Medjugorje (and greater Yugoslavia) have made a postscript necessary.

When the alleged apparitions began in June 1981, few people had heard of the village of Medjugorje in what was then communist Yugoslavia. However, as the apparitions grew in notoriety and some 10 to 15 million people descended on the village in the decade that followed, Medjugorje seemed well on its way to rivaling Lourdes and Fátima as one of the world's most popular Marian shrines.

As of fall 1992, a brutal civil war rages in the breakaway Yugoslav republic of Bosnia-Hercegovina. This bloody conflict has reduced the flow of pilgrims to Medjugorje to a virtual trickle, and streets that once teemed with thousands of Catholic seekers are now virtually empty. While Medjugorje itself has not yet been shelled, much of the nearby city of Mostar, *including the church and home of Medjugorje's fiercest opponent, Bishop Pavao Zanic,* has been devastated. Taking precautions because of nearby fighting, the priests at Medjugorje's St. James Parish have had to say mass in the church's basement, which has been converted to a bomb shelter.[1]

While the war has stopped the massive influx of pilgrims, the four remaining visionaries still claim to receive daily apparitions.

Various miracles are still being reported, but on a much smaller scale. Some of the priests at St. James Parish have stated that the war is the result of people not embracing the apocalyptic message of "Our Lady, Queen of Peace." Father Slavko Barbaric, spiritual adviser to the visionaries, insists that there is some significant message for the world in the fact that the civil war started precisely ten years after the apparitions began in 1981.[2]

Medjugorje generally remains a very popular topic among American Catholics. Books on the apparitions continue to top the Catholic best-seller lists, and Medjugorje conferences in the United States attract thousands.

The armed conflict in the former Yugoslavia has also hampered the investigation of the Yugoslav Bishops Conference, the body responsible for assessing the apparition's validity. Because of the civil war and the complex nature of events in Medjugorje, the Catholic church's official evaluation of Medjugorje may still be many years away.

While an official word from the church may not be coming soon, there is a rising concern about Medjugorje among some Catholic scholars and investigators. The concern centers around a book titled *Poem of the Man-God* by Maria Valtorta, a 1900-page work written in 1947 and first published in Italian. Today a five-volume edition is available in English. *Poem of the Man-God* was considered by its author to be actual revelatory literature about the life of Jesus, received through divine dictation. How is this book connected to Medjugorje? According to visionary Maria Pavlovic, this book was endorsed by the mysterious lady of Medjugorje as good Christian literature. This was confirmed in our personal interview with visionary Vicka Ivankovic who stated "Our Lady" had indeed approved this book to Maria when asked about it (see the interview with Vicka Ivankovic, Appendix A).

The problems with this book are numerous, both from a Catholic and evangelical Protestant point of view. First, while the book claims to be a special revelation about the life of Jesus (Valtorta refers to herself as the "secretary of Jesus"), in several places it actually contradicts what the New Testament teaches about Jesus. In fact, the volume contains significant historical and geographical errors and suggests that the sin of Adam and Eve was sexual in nature (implying that Eve had sex with the serpent, or that the first sin involved masturbation). The book is clearly a vulgar, blasphemous, and fraudulent "revelation." And while a growing number of Catholic scholars have accepted the above charges, they reject the book for yet another reason: Unbeknownst to most Medjugorje supporters, *Poem of the Man-God* was placed on the Vatican's Index of Forbidden Books on December 16, 1959 under the authority of Pope John XXIII. The Vatican newspaper *L'Osservatore Romano* described Valtorta's work as "A Badly Fictionalized Life of Jesus." Further, this official church ban of Valtorta's work was confirmed in 1985 by Joseph Cardinal Ratzinger, the head of the Sacred Congregation for the Doctrine of the Faith.[3]

The dilemma for Medjugorje supporters is obvious: *The Virgin of Medjugorje has approved a work that the Catholic church's magisterium* (official teaching office) *has explicitly condemned!* It would seem that Medjugorje supporters must choose between the lady of Medjugorje or the authority of the pope.

The respondent to our book, Mitchell Pacwa, has denounced *Poem of the Man-God* as a fraudulent and erroneous work. And while he has reserved final judgment on Medjugorje pending the church's official evaluation, he believes that the visionaries are obligated to renounce Valtorta's work. Father Pacwa also leaves the door open to the possibility that one or more of the visionaries (e.g., Maria) may have misunderstood or misinterpreted the apparition's approval of Valtorta's work. Nevertheless, Pacwa maintains that if Medjugorje is to retain credibility as a potentially authentic apparition, then the visionaries must respond in obedience to the church's official teaching and reject the *Poem of the Man-God*.

The authors of this book, however, take a much stronger stand than does Father Pacwa. If the visionaries cannot be trusted to rightly interpret the apparition's messages, then all objectivity is lost and the messages have no objective credibility. On the other hand, Valtorta's revelations are clearly false—just as all so-called revelations are—because the faith has been "once for all" entrusted to the saints (Jude 3). There is no need for further revelations concerning the life of Jesus, because Scripture is God's sole and supreme revelation (1 Cor. 4:6; 2 Tim. 3:16; 2 Peter 1:20, 21).

In addition, the gross exegetical and theological errors found in *Poem of the Man-God* make it apparent that this work is a spiritual fraud. However, there is also evidence that the book may be the product of mediumistic trance-channeling. The fact that Valtorta claimed to receive dictated messages which are incompatible with Scripture from a spiritual source is reason enough to suspect a demonic counterfeit. The evidence that the Medjugorje apparitions are themselves demonic (i.e., unbiblical doctrine and a connection to necromancy), together with the Medjugorje apparition's recommendation of a counterfeit revelation *(Poem of the Man-God)*, give clear signs that the Medjugorje manifestations are a demonic counterfeit.

The words of the apostle John are as appropriate today as the day they were written:

> Dear friends, do not believe every spirit, but test the spirits to see whether they are from God, because many false prophets have gone out into the world (1 John 4:1).

1. Lance Gay, "War drives faithful from shrine," *Rocky Mountain News,* 30 July 1992, p. 4.

2. Ibid.

3. The documentation substantiating these charges was provided by Father Mitchell Pacwa, S.J., Professor of Theology at Loyola University of Chicago. Photocopies of this documentation can be obtained by contacting the Christian Research Institute, P.O. Box 500, San Juan Capistrano, CA 92693 USA. Please enclose a $5 donation for copying and shipping costs.

Bibliography

Catholic Sources

1. Mariology

Abbott, Walter M., ed. *The Documents of Vatican II*. Translated by Joseph Gallagher. New York: Guild Press, 1966.

Attwater, Donald. *A Dictionary of Mary*. New York: P. J. Kennedy and Sons, 1956.

Brown, Raymond E., Karl Donfried, Joseph Fitzmeyer, John Reumann, eds. *Mary in the New Testament*. New York: Paulist Press, 1978.

Carol, Juniper B., ed. *Mariology*. 3 vols. Milwaukee: Bruce Publishing Company, 1955.

————. *Fundamentals of Mariology*. New York: Benziger Bros., 1956.

Congar, Y. *Christ, Our Lady and the Church: The Irenic Theology*. Westminster, Md.: The Newman Press, 1957.

Deiss, Lucien. *Mary, Daughter of Sion*. Collegeville, Minn.: Liturgical Press, 1972.

Denzinger, H., and A. Schonmetzer. *Enchiridion Symbolorum*. Freiburg im Breisgau: Herder, 1965.

Dictionary of Mary. New York: Catholic Book Publishing Company, 1985.

Flannery, Austin, ed. *Vatican Council II: The Conciliar and Post Conciliar Documents*. Northport, N.Y.: Costello Publishing Company, 1975.

Mary in Faith and Life in the New Age of the Church. Dayton, Ohio: International Marian Research Institute, 1983.

179

McHugh, John. *The Mother of Jesus in the New Testament*. Garden City, N.Y.: Doubleday, 1975.

New Catholic Encyclopedia. New York: McGraw-Hill, 1967.

O'Carroll, Michael. *Theotokos: A Theological Encyclopedia of the Blessed Virgin Mary*. Wilmington, Del.: Michael Glazier, 1982.

O'Meara, T. *Mary in Protestant and Catholic Theology*. New York: Sheed & Ward, 1956.

Ott, Ludwig. *Fundamentals of Catholic Dogma*. Rockford, Ill.: TAN Books and Publishers, 1974.

Rahner, Karl. *Mary: Mother of the Lord*. Wheathampstead, Hertfordshire: Anthony Clarke, 1974.

Sheed, F. J. *Theology for Beginners*. 3d ed. Ann Arbor, Mich.: Servant Books, 1981.

2. Apparitions of Mary

Connor, Edward. *Recent Apparitions of Our Lady*. Fresno, Calif.: Academy Guild Press, 1960.

Cranston, Ruth. *The Miracle of Lourdes*. New York: Image Books, Doubleday, 1988.

Estrade, Jean-Pierre. *The Appearances of the Blessed Virgin Mary at the Grotto of Lourdes*. Translated by J. Girolesstrone. Westminster: Art and Book Co., 1912.

Fox, Robert J. *Rediscovering Fatima*. Huntington, Ind.: Our Sunday Visitor, 1982.

Johnston, Francis. *Fatima: The Great Sign*. Rockford, Ill.: TAN Books and Publishers, 1980.

Laurentin, Rene. *Bernadette of Lourdes, A Life Based on Authenticated Documents*. Minneapolis: Winston Press, 1979.

Lochet, Louis. *Apparitions of Our Lady*. New York: Herder and Herder Publishing, 1960.

Odell, Catherine M. *Those Who Saw Her: The Apparitions of Mary*. Huntington, Ind.: Our Sunday Visitor, 1986.

Pelletier, Joseph A. *The Sun Danced at Fatima*. Worcester, Mass.: Assumption Publications, 1951.

Zimdars-Swartz, Sandra L. *Encountering Mary*. Princeton, N.J.: Princeton University Press, 1991.

3. Medjugorje

Belanger, Louis, and Ivo Sivric. *The Hidden Face of Medjugorje.* Vol. 1. Quebec: Editions Psilog, 1989.

Connell, Jan. *Queen of the Cosmos: Interviews with the Visionaries.* Orleans, Mass.: Paraclete Press, 1990.

Craig, Mary. *Spark from Heaven: The Mystery of the Madonna of Medjugorje.* Notre Dame, Ind.: Ave Maria Press, 1988.

Jones, Michael E. *Medjugorje: The Untold Story.* South Bend, Ind.: Fidelity Press, 1988.

Kraljevic, Svetozar. *The Apparitions of Our Lady at Medjugorje.* Edited by Michael Scanlan. Chicago: Franciscan Herald Press, 1984.

Laurentin, Rene. *Eight Years: Latest News of Medjugorje July 1989.* Translated by Juan Gonzales, Jr. Milford, Ohio: The Riehle Foundation, 1989.

———. *Latest News of Medjugorje (June 1987).* Translated by Judith Lohre Stiens. Milford, Ohio: The Riehle Foundation, 1987.

———, and Henri Joyeux. *Scientific and Medical Studies on the Apparitions at Medjugorje.* Dublin: Veritas Publications, 1987.

———, and Ljudevit Rupcic. *Is the Virgin Mary Appearing at Medjugorje?* Translated by Francis Martin. Gaithersburg, Md.: The Word Among Us Press, 1984.

———, and Rene Lejeune. *Messages and Teachings of Mary at Medjugorje.* Translated by Juan Gonzales, Jr. Milford, Ohio: The Riehle Foundation, 1988.

Meyer, Gabriel. *A Portrait of Medjugorje.* Studio City, Calif.: Twin Circle Publishing Company, 1990.

Miravalle, Mark. *Heart of the Message of Medjugorje.* Steubenville, Ohio: Franciscan University Press, 1988.

———. *The Message of Medjugorje: The Marian Message to the Modern World.* New York: University Press of America, 1986.

Weible, Wayne. *Medjugorje: The Message.* Orleans, Mass.: Paraclete Press, 1989.

Protestant Sources (response to Catholic Mariology)

Berkouwer, G. C. *The Conflict with Rome.* Philadelphia: Presbyterian and Reformed Publishing Company, 1958.

———. *The Second Vatican Council and the New Catholicism.* Grand Rapids: William B. Eerdmans Publishing Company, 1965.

Buksbazen, Victor. *Miriam, the Virgin of Nazareth*. Philadelphia: Spearhead Press, 1963.

Carey, George. *A Tale of Two Churches: Can Protestants and Catholics Get Together?* Downers Grove, Ill.: InterVarsity Press, 1984.

Colacci, Mario. *The Doctrinal Conflict Between Roman Catholic and Protestant Christianity*. Minneapolis: T. S. Denison and Company, 1962.

Geisler, Norman L. *Signs and Wonders*. Wheaton, Ill.: Tyndale House Publishers, 1988.

Macquarrie, John. *Mary for All Christians*. Grand Rapids: William B. Eerdmans Publishing Company, 1991.

Pelikan, Jaroslav. *The Riddle of Roman Catholicism*. New York: Abingdon Press, 1959.

Schaff, David S. *Our Fathers' Faith and Ours*. New York: G. P. Putnam's Sons, 1928.

Schrotenboer, Paul G. *Roman Catholicism: A Contemporary Evangelical Perspective*. Grand Rapids: Baker Book House, 1987.

Toon, Peter. *Protestants and Catholics: A Guide to Understanding the Differences among Christians*. Ann Arbor, Mich.: Servant Publications, 1984.

Von Hase, Karl. *Handbook to the Controversy with Rome*. London: The Religious Tract Society, 1906.

Wells, David F. *Revolution in Rome*. Downer's Grove, Ill.: InterVarsity Press, 1972.

Subject Index

Scripture Index